BRIDGE THE GAP

BRIDGE THE GAP

DELIVERING SERMONS THAT LEAD TO CONVERSION RATHER THAN CONFUSION

NICK NEWMAN

ISBN: 9781699000700

For bulk orders please email hello@nicknewman.com
Cover design by Ashley Ulmer Designs
First Edition, Version 1.1

To my wife, Tori, whose sacrifices are unmatched and grace is inspiring, I dedicate this book to you.

TABLE OF CONTENTS

INTRODUCTION

The text message read, "I need to change some things in my life, heading to church tomorrow." Excitement filled me to the core. I had been praying for this friend for over a year. It wasn't uncommon to receive a late night phone call asking for a ride because he was too intoxicated to drive himself. I was there, present, and ready to share the love of Jesus with my friend. He had since gone off to college but distance doesn't refute prayers and it sure doesn't stop the pursuit of God.

This text message filled me with joy because it was a step in the right direction. I thought to myself, "Yes! He is going to church tomorrow." I thanked God and even shared what had happened with the guys in my small group. The next day, it was hard for me to even focus in church and I was on staff. Probably not the best thing to admit, but I was eagerly waiting for the follow up text. We went out to lunch and still nothing, so I initiated the conversation. "Hey man! How was it?" His response broke my heart.

"Honestly, I left more confused. I didn't understand what the guy was talking about. Maybe I just don't belong."

I wish I could tell you that this was an isolated

event. I can't. My heart breaks because there are so many people who leave churches each week not understanding the message they have just heard. Too many people leave feeling like they don't belong because the sermon was delivered at a grade level much higher than theirs.

You may be a pastor, young leader or Sunday school teacher. Know this: eternity is at stake! We do not get to save people. That is the work of God. However, we can make it as easy as possible for people to accept the good news of Jesus Christ. I think most of the time there is a large gap between the messages we write and the audience who receives. This book is designed to help you combat that and deliver messages that communicate the Gospel every time. I believe that through teaching the good news of Jesus in a way that people can understand allows for more people to accept Him as their personal Savior.

I believe that there are some simple, practical, and effective ways to preach which will lead to more conversions and less confusion in the local church. When we begin talking about preaching in a way that captures audiences, some religious leaders get anxious. I'm not going to propose that teaching in a way that tickles ears or waters down scripture is the way to go, I am simply trying to help people leave your church knowing the beauty of the good news of Jesus Christ. My desire is to do whatever I can to bankrupt hell and impact eternity.

You may be wondering why *Bridge the Gap*? A "gap" is a break or hole in an object or between two objects. Gaps are everywhere. In between teeth, on sidewalks, and all throughout life. You may find yourself in a gap in life: a space between your current assignment and your calling. Gaps are a natural part of life. There is a gap we far too often ignore. The gap between where I am and where God wants me to be.

The purpose of this book is to help you learn how to teach in a way that helps people bridge that gap. My hope is that by the end of our journey you communicate with more confidence than you have had. Trusting not in your own abilities, but in God's. You can confidently preach repentance, which is lacking in many local churches knowing that ultimately God sent Jesus so that the gap between us and Him could be mended. You may have read many books on preaching and teaching and have a good grasp on your craft. Perhaps someone has asked you to teach and you have no clue what you are doing. Regardless, I think you will enjoy the simplicity and beauty of the process. It's an honor to journey with you in efforts that more people will surrender their lives to Christ!

SECTION ONE

CHAPTER ONE

CHECK YOUR HEART

"God is most glorified in us when we are most
satisfied in Him."
- John Piper

"... for the mouth speaks what the heart is full of."
- Luke 6:45b NIV

As I started writing this book, it was incredibly difficult to come to terms with what chapter one would be. After all, this is the chapter that I give away for free, and the one you judge to determine if this is a book you deem worthy of a look at the second chapter. It's almost like trying a restaurant on opening night, waiting to see how the service is and how long you have to wait to get your food. Will this be a good experience? I think that is largely up to you.

I want the first thing we dive into in chapter one to be your heart. You may have just let out a deep sigh because you realize your heart has some issues. Know that you are not alone. Jeremiah 17:9 says that our hearts are "wicked and deceitful." Encouraging right? Makes you want to order 500 coffee mugs with "my heart is wicked" plastered on them. It may also shed light as to why "just follow your heart" may actually be the worst advice ever passed down generationally. We all have a heart that I think we know to a small degree is deceitful. Yes, we know that our heart matters, but does it really matter that much in the area of preaching and teaching? I believe it unequivocally does. Jesus says in Luke 6:

"A good person produces good out of the good stored up in his heart. An evil person produces evil out of the

evil stored up in his heart, for his mouth speaks from the overflow of the heart." Luke 6:45 CSB

You have picked up this book, or it was given to you, to elevate your ability to communicate the good news of Jesus Christ. As we speak and teach we must address the condition of our hearts because Jesus says that we speak from the overflow of our **heart**. He doesn't say, "...from the overflow of your talent, education, anointing, or wealth the mouth speaks..." It's your heart. Examining your heart reveals every impurity that lays beneath the surface of our own lives.

I will never forget one day when a high school football coach of mine, Mike Johns (still a legend in my mind) had an illustration for us. He was talking about life, the ups, downs, and turns of this crazy roller-coaster-like endeavor. In one hand he had an orange which he tossed as he talked and then suddenly he squeezed it as hard as he could. As he squeezed, everything inside of the orange spilled out. Then, with a smile on his face, he said, "What is in you will always come out of you when you get squeezed." The moment you sign up to proclaim God's truth to people, know that you will be squeezed. It is not a matter of *if* you will be squeezed but rather **when**. The enemy will launch a full scale attack against you and your loved ones and make no mistake, whatever is inside of you will spill out everywhere.

INSECURITY

I started in ministry at 18 years old and early on I felt as if this dark cloud followed me everywhere. I was confident and excited for God's unique plan for my life, until I got around other people in ministry. As soon as I met another pastor or church leader I started to clam up. Something inside me would bubble up and I would feel the need to shift the focus back onto myself. Maybe if I just told them a little more about me then it would show that God was doing amazing things in my life. I wanted to impress people. I wanted to be liked, longed for, and adored.

Truth is, I was insecure. I had bought into the crafty voice of the enemy who had no problem reminding me of the following:

You graduated High School with a .4 GPA.
You have had a laundry list of drug charges.
You dropped out of college.
You have only been following Jesus for a short amount of time.
You aren't good enough or even cut out for this.

Insecurities are one of those things that everyone

deals with. They disappear but tend to bubble up to the surface every now and then. Recently, I was having a conversation with someone on our team and afterwards I had that gross insecure feeling from so many years ago. I asked the Lord to give me fresh insight, show me the dangers, and help me walk in freedom. Ask and you shall receive! The Lord started showing me things in the life of Peter.

Let me set the scene for you: a group of men have just come in from a long day of ministry. The table has been prepared for them; it's a dinner party of sorts. This party, though, doesn't have the happiest of conversations. In the middle of the dinner, amongst small talk, an interruption occurs. Jesus has tapped His glass to walk the disciples through communion, but then things got awkward. He looks to Judas and says, "I know you will betray Me." After this, the disciples are focused on Judas until they head to the Mount of Olives and Jesus shifts the attention to Peter telling him that he would be the one to deny Him. Peter responds quickly to Jesus, "Even if all fall away on account of You, I never will" (Matthew 26:33).

Jesus assures Peter that He has the whole God thing going on and isn't wrong about what Peter will do. (Good news for them, they will have the chance to talk about it on the shore of a beach later on.) They head to the Garden of Gethsemane for Jesus to pray. Jesus prays; the disciples sleep; Jesus wakes them, and the cycle continues until Judas arrives. He is not alone though. Judas has brought guards to arrest Jesus and so the words spoken at dinner come to pass. Jesus has resolved in His heart that this is the way it has to be, but not everyone feels the same. As the guards stand in front of Jesus something crazy happens:

> *Then Simon Peter drew a sword and slashed off the right ear of Malchus, the high priest's slave. But Jesus said to Peter, "Put your sword back into its sheath. Shall I not drink from the cup of suffering the Father has given me?"*
> *John 18:10-11 NLT*

The sequence of events is no coincidence. Peter finds out that he may betray Jesus and he can't stay awake in the garden, and now people have come to arrest Jesus. Peter looks at the situation and sees the opportunity he has been waiting for. This is his shot to prove to Jesus and the rest of the team that he would never take his jersey off. How can he prove it? By attacking the man coming after Jesus.

Insecurity causes Peter to try and prove his worth to his brothers and to Jesus. Make no mistake, you will always wound others trying to prove your worth to the team. Don't allow your insecurity to bring you to the place where you wound others. If you need to preach in order to feel useful to God then you don't need to preach. God doesn't need you, He chooses you. Find security in your unique design and God's love for you. An identity rooted in Him is crucial for you as a communicator. You are a son or daughter of the Creator of the universe. This family isn't one you buy entrance into, but one that you were bought into by the payment of Jesus!

"
YOU WILL ALWAYS WOUND OTHERS TRYING TO PROVE YOUR WORTH TO THE TEAM.

SELF-EXAMINATION
One of the things that has been so beneficial for

me in life and ministry is taking advantage of an opportunity to pause and ask myself questions. It is in those moments of answering that my heart is revealed. So let me ask you this: **why do you want to be better at teaching and preaching?** You may be thinking, "how dare he question the motivation of my heart in this," but breathe for a second. I am just trying to deliver some fresh accountability into your walk with Christ.

Accountability may feel like a personal attack if you aren't willing or ready to deal with your toxic heart issues. I would encourage you to sit alone with the Lord for a moment with Psalm 26:2 "Put me on trial, LORD, and cross-examine me. Test my motives and my heart." When I sat down and assessed the motives of my heart for wanting to be a better communicator I didn't like what I saw. On the surface, I had this beautiful answer filled with "Christianese" (If you aren't familiar, that's the language Christians use to let you know in just a few sentences how spiritual they are). My surface level answer was, "lost people, I want to see lost people saved." But truthfully, deep down it went a little something like this:

"Being better at communicating means
bigger spotlight, and spotlight means
influence, and influence means

more people meet Jesus."

My heart revealed that I wasn't as concerned with people meeting Jesus as I was with them knowing me. In the arena of my own heart, I came first and Jesus came second. That is a major problem. A big spotlight might be something that the Lord gives someone, but if spotlight is your motivation, that disqualifies you. Preaching becomes performance when it's done for the purpose of spotlight.

"PREACHING BECOMES PERFORMANCE WHEN IT'S DONE FOR THE PURPOSE OF SPOTLIGHT.

I would venture to guess that I am not alone in my desire for the spotlight. Maybe you find yourself in a similar spot. Maybe you aren't willing to ask yourself the question for fear of the answers. God isn't shocked or surprised at what you uncover. In fact, 1 Corinthians 4:5 says He "reveals the motives of the heart." Regardless of what you uncover, there is hope! We serve a God who corrects and purifies motives of the heart, bringing healing and wholeness.

I would encourage you to sit before the Lord with the same declaration as David, "Search me O' God." Thankfully, we have a God who knows our issues even before we discover them. He delights in revealing anything that stands in the way of our relationship with Him. Know this, as you deep dive into your heart, or just in your everyday life, you may discover heart issues that aren't pretty. God isn't scared of them. He is willing and ready to help you walk in freedom to become more like Jesus. It's a process; trust the process.

CHECK ENGINE LIGHT

Around 1974 the check engine light was invented by Chrysler. Back then, there was something on the odometer that would say, "Check EGR." Today, it is a symbol that lights up on your dash, notifying you of a pending problem. If you drive a car made since the 2000's it is standard to have a check engine light. I know for certain that my car has one because sometimes I ignore it. Why would I ignore the check engine light? It may be due to not wanting to address the problem, feeling like it's insignificant, or not having the money to fix it. I have learned the hard way that just because you ignore it doesn't mean it isn't there.

I believe that God has given you and I the gift of the Holy Spirit to act as the check engine light of our soul. As you dive into this book think about the issues of your heart. You are not alone. I have my own issues to deal with and I have to do just that, deal with them. God designed you and I to grow in our relationship with Him, but that doesn't happen by ignoring your check engine light. When God highlights an area of your heart that needs to be addressed, pull your car into the bay of your Creator. Allow God to heal, purify, and redeem that which doesn't reflect Him. This isn't something that is just beneficial for you as a communicator, but as a son or daughter of God. When God reveals something, know that He knows what is best for you! Warning, choosing not to check the engine light of your heart may result in the loss of an ear for someone around you.

CHAPTER TWO

KNOW YOUR ROLE

"Where I found truth, there found I my God, who is the
truth itself."
- Augustine

"He determines the number of the stars; he gives to all
of them their names. Great is our Lord, and abundant in
power; his understanding is beyond measure."
- Psalm 147:4-5 ESV

Where do you turn when looking for answers? Do you call up a friend, mentor, or schedule a meeting with your pastor? Maybe you create a poll on social media to figure out what direction to go. I have found that as a follower of Jesus, there is no better source for a solution than scripture. I believe that there is wisdom in people, but when you are deep-diving into the issues of your own heart, the first source we must turn to is God. As I was assessing my motivation for wanting to become a better communicator, here is what the Lord showed me in John 1:

And this is the testimony of John, when the Jews sent priests and Levites from Jerusalem to ask him, "Who are you?" He confessed, and did not deny, but confessed, "I am not the Christ." And they asked him, "What then? Are you Elijah?" He said, "I am not." "Are you the Prophet?" And he answered, "No." So they said to him, "Who are you? We need to give an answer to those who sent us. What do you say about yourself?" He said, "I am the voice of one crying out in the wilderness, 'Make straight the way of the Lord,' as the prophet Isaiah said." They asked him, "Then why are you baptizing, if you are neither the Christ, nor Elijah, nor the Prophet?" John answered them, "I baptize with water, but among you stands one you do not know, even he who comes after me, the strap of whose sandal I am not worthy to untie." These things took place

in Bethany across the Jordan, where John was baptizing.
John 1:19-28 ESV

How do you deal with the pride-bend of your heart in the area of preaching? The first step is understanding that your role and position is that of John the Baptist, not Jesus. Knowing your role in the narrative of God's redemptive plan for the world is crucial to helping your heart become pure.

John is standing in a crowd of confused religious leaders and from the beginning is saying, "I am not the Christ." To grasp the meaning of what John has stated I think you have to look at the Greek word for Christ; "Christos," a Greek word meaning "anointed one." Anointing was the pouring out of oil by priests, it was also done to mark the one who was to be king. I believe that what John is saying is this: "I am not the king God has promised to send to you."

Let this embed itself into the fabric of your heart. As the crowd is trying to figure out if John is their Savior, he says, "Nope, I am simply making way for the One who is coming." John understood his position inside of the Kingdom of God and wanted to make sure that he made it clear to others what his role was as well. Was it to be the Savior? Nope, Jesus is on the way and once you see Him, everything changes.

There are so many hats I wear as a pastor and

teacher of God's Word, but the one that has transcended all titles is "waymaker." When my heart came to grips with the fact that I am making way for Christ, it set me free in two areas. First, I no longer had to carry the weight of saving people. There was a season of my life where I thought that if I wasn't perfect and didn't knock it out of the park on a Sunday, then lost people went to Hell because of me. Ego check: you and I are not that important. Salvation never has and never will be based on human effort, deeds, or performance. Secondly, it allowed me to have a proper perspective of my role in God's master plan of communication to His people. I don't have to save people. I have the honor of pointing them to the one who came and died in their place so that they may have life abundantly!

Every Sunday, before I walk on stage to teach, I give myself a little pep talk, and in wrapping it up, I remind myself "Nick, you are not the Savior, but you know Him. Today, tell them about Him." The win of whatever message you deliver should be that you made way for the Lord to come. Stop carrying the weight of saving people and start paving the way for people to see the King who has already come!

From the point of birth, we enter into a broken and fallen world. Our lives are filled with chaos externally, but internally, there is the same thing. Hardwired into the fiber of our being is the longing for a king who will restore order and make things whole. As you are doing the work of the Lord, people may think highly of you or place you on a pedestal. I don't think most people do this on purpose or have malicious intent. They simply can't reconcile within themselves that Jesus is the only king who can bring order. So rather than believe the invisible, they look to the man or woman of God with their broken heart and cry "help me." Unfortunately, most of the time rather than seeing Christ in us, they just see us.

I wish that I could insert a persuasive paragraph that gave you and I the tools to combat the pedestal people put communicators of the Gospel on. However, people throughout scripture looked to things and kings rather than God. People may place you on a pedestal, but your actions determine whether or not you accept the position or step down from it. I don't know if this problem will go away, but understanding your role can give you peace in knowing your motives when others question it. Throughout the next few pages, I will dive into our role and God's in some practical ways!

GOD'S ROLE

I often use this word in the leadership lessons I teach: capacity. If you look at a glass jar, it has a specified capacity. There is a limited amount of things it can do and hold due to its creation and construction. You are the glass jar. You have a specific capacity which is filled by your gifts, abilities, and life. You and I must realize that no matter how much we may want to, we will never have the capacity of God. I think to understand someone's role you look at their design. God, by design, exists in three parts, known as the Trinity: Father, Son, and Spirit

God the Father's primary role is love. One of the most iconic verses in the Bible is John 3:16 "For God so loved the world that He gave His one and only Son, that whoever believes in Him shall not perish but have eternal life." Love isn't something that God does, it's who He is. You have a Heavenly Father who loved you so much that He would send His Son to die in your place. To take it a step further, the people that will listen to you communicate The Gospel need to know that they have a Heavenly Father who loves them that much. The function of the Father is to love.

If I try and fulfill the role of love without God, it won't work. My love tends to be limited and based on human effort. God's love, however, has never been and will never be about performance. "We love because He first loved us" (1 John 4:19).

My ability to love flows from the source of my

Heavenly Father. He first loved me, I experienced that love, and now I can love others. If the order goes any other way I will try and fill a role I was never designed to fill. God is love!

"GOD'S LOVE HAS NEVER BEEN AND WILL NEVER BE ABOUT PERFORMANCE.

The second part of the Trinity is God the Son. We know that God the Father sent His Son (Jesus) into the world not to condemn the world, but to save it (John 3:17)! Yes, Jesus gave us a model for how to treat others, but His primary purpose was dying in our place. Salvation and reconciliation to God come from no one other than Jesus.

"Jesus said to him, "I am the way, and the truth, and the life. No one comes to the Father except through me." John 14:6 ESV

Jesus is the only way to have access to the Father. Unfortunately, most people still treat pastors like the priests of the Old Testament. Back then, the priest was the only one who got to have access to God. People would give sacrifices, and then the priest enters the Holy of Holies to come back with a word for the people from God. Sound familiar? If you're not careful, that's what your teaching will become. Thankfully, the veil between us and God has been torn! There is no longer a separation because of Christ's death on the cross. People need to know that you aren't the Savior and that they have the same access to God, through Christ, as you do!

The last role I want to discuss is the role of the Holy Spirit, which is conviction. Conviction, as defined by the world, is to be found guilty or to receive a guilty verdict. However, that is not the role of the Holy Spirit. Conviction of the Holy Spirit is the gift from God that swoops in to expose evil and shed light onto the things that are unholy. Conviction is the drawing and prompting of God, ushering us to Himself for repentance.

"When the Spirit of truth comes, he will [reveal] all the truth, for he will not speak on his own authority, but whatever he hears he will speak, and he will declare to you the things that are to come" John 16:13 ESV

The Holy Spirit reveals truth. God's delivery mechanism of truth to the world is His Spirit! We don't have to carry the weight of revealing the truth to people; we have the privilege of delivering it. Man-made conviction leads us into the presence of legalism, not freedom. Allow the Holy Spirit to reveal truth at the time He deems fit. I can promise you one thing, God loves the people listening to your sermon way more than you ever could. He knows their names (Jeremiah 1:5), the number of hairs on their head (Luke 12:7), and their hearts (1 Samuel 16:7). If there is anyone qualified to deliver a truth bomb, it's God the Holy Spirit!

Am I saying that God has no other functions? Absolutely not. I hope to show you, on a small scale, the role God plays to help you better understand common pitfalls in preaching.

I have a firm belief in these three things:

1. God is the ultimate source of love. Every ounce of love that I can produce flows from Him.

If I am the source of love- I will exert all of my energy in loving others until I have nothing left. There is no need for a relationship with God.

2. God is the only one with the ability to save. He died for people, and I don't have to.

If I think I can save- I will draw people to myself, giving them false hope. They don't need me; they need Jesus. I fail, but He NEVER does!

3. God is the deliverer of conviction. He knows what people need to hear, and when they need to hear it.

If I try to bring conviction- I will let pride bring me to the place where I think I can do God's job better than He does — pushing people to places in my timing rather than God's.

These roles of God encompass the full truth which we should be shouting from the rooftops! God loves us enough that despite our faults, flaws, and failures, He made a way for us to have a relationship with Him. He did that by sending Jesus to live a sinless life, and ultimately die the death we deserved to die. Yep, God sent His own Son so that, through His death, we might be reconciled. By placing your belief in Him, you have access to God, and He has a gift for you! The Holy Spirit. It's not spooky or mystic, it is the empowerment of God to live out your everyday life growing in your relationship with Him.

God has been fulfilling these roles long before I even breathed my first breath. Let us recognize the beauty of our God and the roles that He plays. Perhaps one of the best things that you could do right now is take a moment and hit the pause button. Stop, remember, and thank God for who He is. He is a lover of people, Savior of the world, and convictor of righteousness. Thank you, God, for the role You play.

OUR ROLE

After looking at some of the roles God plays, it can quickly feel like there is nothing left for you. Like a child at Christmas watching everyone open gifts but seeing nothing with your name, you say, "what about me?" Know that you have a role to play and you have not been forgotten. God, since the very beginning of time, has used people to forward His mission and advance His Kingdom. Adam received a job to steward the Kingdom of God before the fall, not after. This shows me that part of God's perfect plan involves you and I partnering with Him!

There is something powerful about the instructions of a mentor. In 2 Timothy, we find Paul writing to a young pastor and leader that he has spent years investing into, and says, "Hey, be sure to share what I'm about to teach you, it's so good" (typical pastor). Then he writes:

> "Endure suffering along with me, as a good soldier of Christ Jesus. Soldiers don't get tied up in the affairs of civilian life, for then they cannot please the officer who enlisted them. And athletes cannot win the prize unless they follow the rules. And hardworking farmers should be the first to enjoy the fruit of their labor."
> 2 Timothy 2:3-6 NLT

Paul gives Timothy three distinct figures to model himself after. In three short verses, he says, "Timothy, don't forget that God has called you to be a soldier, an athlete, and a farmer." I think Paul would tell us the same thing.

The first role that we see is that of a soldier (v3). As a soldier, I think you need to know that you signed up for battle. A soldier doesn't get to a battlefield, and say, "Nope, not what I signed up for" when bullets start flying. In the same way, when you decide to communicate the Gospel, the powers of Hell launch a full assault on you. The spiritual warfare you will face and endure as a communicator is not for the faint of heart. Thankfully, Isaiah 54:17 declares that "no weapon formed against us will prosper." It doesn't say that weapons won't form, it says they won't prosper. Don't ignore the spiritual warfare you face. Confront it, fight it, knowing that He that is in you is greater than anything in the world.

A soldier signs up to fight, but they also sign up to be about the king's business. When you sign up to deliver the Gospel, my encouragement to you is to lay down your agenda and self-centered motives. If you are teaching God's Word for attention or the approval of man, please step out now before people get hurt in your pursuit of fulfillment. In Galatians 1:10, Paul shows us that it's impossible to do this for the approval of man and God at the same time. Maybe you wonder, what's the King's business? From Genesis 3 to now, God has been in the business of reconciling people to Himself. His end game is that none would perish (2 Peter 3:9), but have everlasting life through Christ. Your heart will come alive as you embrace God's heart as your own.

The next person Paul brings into the picture is an athlete (v5). One of the things I love about athletes is their dedication to improving. So many people who teach God's Word disqualify themselves due to a lack of involvement in the process of sanctification. Just as an athlete goes to the gym to train, God desires to stretch your spiritual muscles. When things get complicated the natural tendency is to slow down or quit. The key to longevity in being used by God is perseverance. Yes, things will get difficult, but never forget that God is with you and for you! Be encouraged by James 1:12, "Blessed is the one who perseveres under trial because, having stood the test, that person will receive the crown of life that the Lord has promised to those who love Him."

The willingness to push through hard things is vital, but it's also essential to have discipline. The unfortunate downfall of ministry is that it's easier to become so busy with the work, that you neglect your relationship with God. To last as a communicator of the Gospel, you must develop some disciplines for how you spend time. Spending time with God through prayer and reading scripture is one of the ways that you remain devoted to your relationship with Him. I can't have a relationship with someone I never spend time with or talk to. Discipline is not an accidental investment, it's an intentional one! Make the conscious choice to pursue and develop your relationship with God.

Last, Paul says to be like a hardworking farmer (v6). The church my wife and I started is in a small farming community in North Carolina has a population of 1,800 people, and no I didn't forget a zero. In this town I have had the opportunity to chat with many farmers, and I have come to have a deeper appreciation for the art of seed planting. Planting isn't for the faint of heart. It's a task that requires you to exert energy on the front end in hopes that one day you might reap a harvest.

> *"I planted the seed, Apollos watered it, but God has been making it grow. So neither the one who plants nor the one who waters is anything, but only God, who makes things grow. The one who plants and the one who waters have one purpose, and they will each be rewarded according to their own labor." 1 Corinthians 3:6-8 NIV*

Paul understood that his role was to plant. Someone else might come through and water, but it was ultimately God's responsibility to grow it as He saw fit. Next time you get so eager to build your church or ministry, remember growth is not your job, seed planting is!

As verse 6 comes to an end, Paul says that the farmer should enjoy their hard work. Maybe you are around a different group of ministry leaders than I am, but I see so many people who teach God's Word that lack one crucial thing: joy. Not the put a fake smile on or the "fake it til' ya make it" stuff, but pure, genuine excitement for the opportunity to plant seeds in the gardens of our Heavenly Father. A farmer can't only focus on the harvest, or he will only have food for a season. I think the best thing you can do is spend your life planting seeds for the next generation to harvest. I am called to be a seed planter and take joy in it! Inevitably when those thoughts or feelings arise and I feel discouraged, I turn to this verse:

"Therefore, my beloved brothers, be steadfast, immovable, always abounding in the work of the Lord, knowing that in the Lord your labor is not in vain."
1 Corinthians 15:58 ESV

I pray that you have a better understanding of your role and God's! He is the source of love and I have signed up for His agenda. He has the ability to save and I am dedicated to seeing people saved by Him. He is the one who convicts and I am a seed planter who enjoys working for the Lord. Knowing God's role and yours can set you free from carrying a weight only God can carry.

" KNOWING GOD'S ROLE AND YOURS CAN SET YOU FREE FROM CARRYING A WEIGHT ONLY GOD CAN CARRY.

CHAPTER THREE

THE GREAT DIVIDE

"You're born. You suffer. You die. Fortunately,
there's a loophole."
- Billy Graham

"For God so loved the world that he gave his one and
only Son, that whoever believes in him shall not perish
but have eternal life."
- John 3:16 NIV

Have you ever found there to be a great distance between where you are and where you want to be? You find yourself single, but have a desire for someone to like it enough to put a ring on it. Maybe you are currently overweight and have a big goal for what you want to lose. There is the reality of where you are, followed by the understanding of where you could be.

The space between where we are and where we want to be is a gap. We see and know that there are gaps all around us. In fact, gaps formed in the heart of every person after the most tragic event that has ever occurred. While events like 9/11 or Sandyhook shook the nation to its core, only one event's effects have carried through every generation. You may have guessed it by now, it's the fall of man in Genesis 3.

In the beginning, God creates. Genesis 1 is all about the magnificence and power of our God. He has the ability at the utterance of a word to speak things into existence. Toward the end of the chapter, God creates man in His image (v27) and realizes he is weird and shouldn't be alone in Genesis 2:18. He gives them one thing to not do: eat from the tree of the knowledge of good and evil. Once the serpent started whispering into the ear of Eve, the temptation grew stronger and stronger, leading to a choice. Much like a cookie jar with "do not touch" Eve reached her hand into the tree, grabbed the fruit, and took a bite.

She then looks at her husband, Adam, and offers him the same fruit. He bites into it and Genesis 3:7 says, "Then the eyes of both of them were opened, and they realized they were naked; so they sewed fig leaves together and made coverings for themselves." Shame enters into the picture at this moment and they have a new revelation of their existence. Something has changed and we are about to see it come with full force. God is coming back for an afternoon stroll.

"Then the man and his wife heard the sound of the Lord God as he was walking in the garden in the cool of the day, and they hid from the Lord God among the trees of the garden. But the Lord God called to the man, "Where are you?" Genesis 3:8-9 NLT

If God is all-knowing, then why in the world would He ask Adam where he is? For the first time, but indeed not the last time, a gap has been created. Isaiah 59:2 shows us that sin creates a separation between God and man. It wasn't that God lost Adam; God simply is too holy to coexist with sin. Adam and Eve's choice landed them in a place where there was a gap between them and God.

The separation between God and us was man-made, not God-designed. God designed you and I to live in perfection with Him, to walk, talk, and enjoy life with Him. But now, due to effects of sin, there is a gap. God wasn't satisfied with separation because He created us gapless.

As we continue reading in Genesis 3, God reveals what life now looks like because of sin. What a bummer, but yes our actions do have consequences. Then we get to my favorite part of Genesis chapter 3. Tucked into one tiny verse is the full beauty of the Gospel.

"The Lord God made garments of animal skin for Adam and his wife and clothed them." Genesis 3:21 NLT

That whole verse is how God mends the gap for us. Here are three things to pull from that verse:

1. Adam's clothing wasn't sufficient- Adam had already covered himself with fig leaves, but God made him and Eve a new set of clothing. Only God can cover your sin.

2. God sacrificed an animal- For Adam and Eve to get this new clothing, an animal had to be sacrificed. Did the animal desire to die? No. Neither did Jesus, yet He dies in our place.

3. The Bloodshed of Jesus covers our sin- Adam and Eve needed to be covered, and God used an animal in Genesis 3 to point us to Jesus. Through the bloodshed of Jesus on the cross, our sin can be covered by the grace of God.

The good news of the Gospel is that God mends the gap between Him and us by sending Jesus to die in our place! That's the beauty of what you and I get to teach every weekend. Through Jesus and only Jesus, the gap between you and God can be bridged. Friends, that is really good news!

The purpose of this book is to help you learn how to bridge that gap in your messages. I think you can learn how to communicate in such a way that each weekend you can stand on stage with confidence. Trusting not in your abilities, but God's. You can confidently preach repentance, which can be a daunting task for a new communicator. But first, I want to lay out the concept for you. You may have read many books on preaching and teaching and have a good grasp on your craft. However, you may be on the other end. Someone has asked you to teach and you have no clue what you are doing. Regardless, I think you will enjoy the simplicity and beauty of the process.

VISUAL ILLUSTRATION - THE GAP

From the onset of this book, I have desired to create something super practical; a guide for you to follow in the message preparation process that will bring focus and clarity to your content. Something that will help you connect with your audience and show them that, in Christ, they can walk in God's preferred future! Below, I have given you the diagram for the premise of this book.

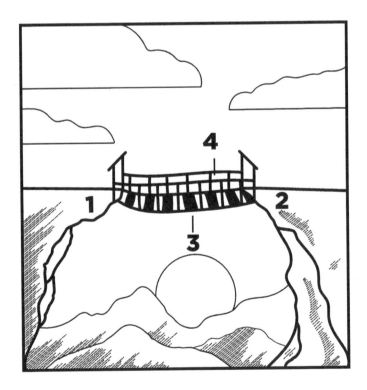

There are four components to this:

1. Where people are (Connection)
2. Where God wants them to be (Vision)
3. Planks (Points and Application)
4. Ropes (Jesus)

I believe that this is the foundational message of the Gospel of Jesus Christ and a method that God used throughout scripture. I believe that God desires to speak to His creation in a way that shows them, 'I understand where you are, but what I have for you is so much better. By being in a relationship with My Son, what once seemed impossible is now possible.' Let me show you this concept fleshed out in scripture:

"As Jesus was starting out on his way to Jerusalem, a man came running up to him, knelt down, and asked, "Good Teacher, what must I do to inherit eternal life?" "Why do you call me good?" Jesus asked. "Only God is truly good. But to answer your question, you know the commandments: 'You must not murder. You must not commit adultery. You must not steal. You must not testify falsely. You must not cheat anyone. Honor your father and mother.' "Teacher," the man replied, "I've obeyed all these commandments since I was young." Looking at the man, Jesus felt genuine love for him. "There is still one

thing you haven't done," he told him. "Go and sell all your possessions and give the money to the poor, and you will have treasure in heaven. Then come, follow me." At this the man's face fell, and he went away sad, for he had many possessions. Jesus looked around and said to his disciples, "How hard it is for the rich to enter the Kingdom of God!" This amazed them. But Jesus said again, "Dear children, it is very hard to enter the Kingdom of God. In fact, it is easier for a camel to go through the eye of a needle than for a rich person to enter the Kingdom of God!" The disciples were astounded. "Then who in the world can be saved?" they asked. Jesus looked at them intently and said, "Humanly speaking, it is impossible. But not with God. Everything is possible with God." Then Peter began to speak up. "We've given up everything to follow you," he said. "Yes," Jesus replied, "and I assure you that everyone who has given up house or brothers or sisters or mother or father or children or property, for my sake and for the Good News, will receive now in return a hundred times as many houses, brothers, sisters, mothers, children, and property—along with persecution. And in the world to come that person will have eternal life. But many who are the greatest now will be least important then, and those who seem least important now will be the greatest then." Mark 10:17-31 NLT

At the start of our story, we find a rich young ruler who has an encounter with Jesus. I think it's interesting that the man has all of the right things going on in this passage of scripture.

First, he runs to Jesus (v17). In this culture, running showed a sense of urgency that men didn't display. We see a man who is in pursuit of Jesus, and that is a great start! Second, he bows down before Jesus. This posture is the acknowledgment of who is in charge in this scenario. No doubt his decision to bow before Jesus is to declare Him an authoritative figure. Last, the man asks some great questions. He doesn't just bow down, but there are some things on this man's heart, and he brings them to someone who can give answers that bring fulfillment.

From the outside looking in, it appears that this young man has it all together. He is pursuing Jesus, bowing before Him, and asking questions. This guy could lead a small group in most churches, but we see some significant discrepancies in his thought process. He asks the question at the end of verse 17, "Good Teacher, what must I do to inherit eternal life?" We see Jesus quickly respond: "Just keep all the commandments."

The young ruler steps to the side and begins to take inventory of his life. Commandment by commandment, he goes down the list checking each one of them off. He hurries back to Jesus not wanting to waste his time and shouts, "I'm good, I've kept all the commandments since I was young" (v20). This young man got so caught up in his head that the only perfect person who has ever walked this earth is standing before him, and yet he says, 'I'm good.'

I want to think that this is an isolated event, but I think this conversation looks a whole lot like what many of our conversations with God will look like when we stand before Him. Some will say things like 'I am a good person, I fed the homeless multiple times a week, I went to church consistently... I'm good.' Jesus wanted him to realize at that moment that he was not good, but a sinner (Romans 3:23).

Jesus continues to look at him and the text says, "Jesus felt genuine love for him." Jesus felt this way because His desire is that none would perish (2 Peter 3:9). With the current thought process of this man, he will stand before Jesus to say "I'm good." Jesus' response will be, "Turn from Me, I never knew you" (Matthew 7:21-23). This man may have missed the mark the first time, but Jesus gave him another shot!

Jesus cast the net out again to this man's heart by saying, "There is still one thing you haven't done." Notice He doesn't rebuke the man, call him a fool, or banish him. Jesus wants to connect with him before He corrects him. He then deep dives into the heart condition of this man and reveals that there is an issue with possessions. Jesus pushes past the surface level and proposes that the king of this man's heart is his stuff. Jesus said, 'sell your stuff, then come follow me' (v21).

"At this the man's face fell, and he went away sad, for he had many possessions." Mark 10:22 NLT

The man left that day filled with sadness because he wasn't willing to surrender everything to God. We don't know what happens to this young ruler, but unless his heart position shifted, he didn't receive salvation. My heart breaks for people like this man who will never know that what God has for them is more significant than anything this world has to offer.

Did you catch the gap? There is a distance between where this young man is, compared to where God desired him to be. I want to show you a simple sermon outline I would use to teach this passage of scripture using the "bridge the gap" concept.

Message title: One Thing You Lack
Scripture: Mark 10:17-31

Where you are - You have something in your life that you haven't given God control of.

Where God wants you to be - Following Him wholeheartedly.

Ropes (Jesus) - Jesus came because we aren't good enough.

Planks (Points and Application) - We will never be good enough. God loves us too much to not call out issues in our lives. Joy comes from surrender. With God, all things are possible.

Preaching Outline:

Introduction - You have something in your life holding you back.

Read Mark 10:17-20

1. We will never be good enough.
Read Romans 3:23

2. God loves us too much to not call out issues in our lives.
Read Mark 10:21

3. Joy comes from surrender.
Read Mark 10:22

4. With God, all things are possible.
Read Mark 10:27

Salvation Prayer

You may be thinking, that isn't actually a sermon outline that he would use, but it is. I simply went into my Google Drive and grabbed an outline to show you this principle. This method of preaching is what I have been using for years, what I use to train communicators on our team, and one I have shared with countless new pastors. I believe that preaching has become more complicated than it has to be. What if each week, as you were led by the Spirit, you bridged the gap for people? What if there was a way to teach that ensured every time you:

1. Connected with them wherever they are.

2. Gave them vision for where God wants them, and helped them see it.

3. Showed them that God's Word still applies to their everyday life.

4. Proclaimed that the only way this is possible is with Jesus.

That's why I wrote this book, and I am honored to have you journey through it with me. Over the next few chapters, we will break down each one of the four components and then together, we will go through how to build messages! I pray that God speaks to you louder than ever as you revel in the beauty of the gap He bridged for you.

"THE GOOD NEWS OF THE GOSPEL IS THAT GOD MENDS THE GAP BETWEEN US AND HIM BY SENDING JESUS TO DIE IN OUR PLACE.

SECTION TWO

CHAPTER FOUR

WHERE YOU ARE
(CONNECTION)

"Jesus is not the man at the top of the stairs—he is the man at the bottom. The friend of sinners. The Savior of those in need of one. Which is all of us—all of the time!"
- Tullian Tchividjian

"I have come into the world as light, so that whoever believes in me may not remain in darkness."
- John 12:46 NIV

Over the last few years, I have watched something shift in our culture with the growing popularity of YouTube. I have grown tremendously just by watching video tutorials on how to do things. Heck, I even learned graphic design and built a successful business from watching videos online. Times have changed.

However, there is one thing I have never been able to learn online: the ability to work on vehicles. You may be thinking, "someone needs to take his man card." You can have it, I won't fight you. Just know that if you take it, you owe me a free oil change because, seriously, I don't know how to do it. There is a reason that I have AAA's car service because if I break down, I am going to need some major help.

One day, I was trying my hardest to fix something on my car. I watched the videos, even followed the advice of some online forums, but nothing was working. Honestly, I was angry, and something inside of me felt like this was my shot to prove something. I realized, though, this was beyond my ability to repair. However, I knew the perfect person to fix it. My dad! Growing up, I watched him fix all sorts of things, and I knew that if anyone could fix it, it would be him. So I swallowed my pride, accepted defeat, and made the phone call. My dad was so excited not only to hear from me, but because I only lived

20 minutes away, let me know that he was coming over. (Side note which has nothing to do with the purpose of the story: what brings you frustration is the very thing that brings others joy. Don't do life alone!) Dad came over with parts in hand, ready to fix it. The hood was lifted, a few minutes went by, he closed the hood, smiled, and said: "It's finished." To which I responded, "Really? Are you sure about that?" Confidently, he invited me to turn the key and, much to my surprise, it cranked right up. That day my car got fixed, and I saw the Gospel unfold right before my eyes. Here are a few things I saw that day:

1. There was a problem that I couldn't fix myself - My car was broken and I couldn't fix it on my own. I realized that I needed someone else to fix it. In the same way, our sin created a debt that we do not have the ability to cover.

2. My father came to me - Broken cars don't drive well. I couldn't just bring the car over to my dad, so he came to me. In the same way, God sent Jesus to come into this world for us!

3. He covered the cost - My dad showed up with the parts in hand to fix the broken condition of my car. There was nothing I had to bring to the table for it to get fixed. In the same way, God covered the entire debt we have because of sin, through Jesus.

Paul wrote it this way:

"But God showed his great love for us by sending Christ to die for us while we were still sinners." Romans 5:8 NLT

You may be familiar with the Gospel, but I want you to let that sink in for just a minute. In the middle of your sin, flaws, and mistakes, God would choose to come die In your place! Rest in that for a moment. Put the book down if you have to, but never forget the beauty of God meeting you where you are.

There is power in remembering that God meets us where we are, and I think people need to be reminded of that. The enemy would love to make people feel like God doesn't understand what they're going through. My concern is that most pastors teach as if their backs are turned to the audience and they are teaching to their seminary professors. It feels cold, and so educated that the average person deducts that God isn't for them. I believe there is a way to make your audience understand that God meets them wherever they currently are, without sacrificing depth in scripture.

"NEVER FORGET THE BEAUTY OF GOD MEETING YOU WHERE YOU ARE.

UNDERSTAND YOUR AUDIENCE

When communicating the good news of Jesus, it's essential to meet people where they are. After all, it is precisely what God did for you and me. If people can't see that God meets them where they are, they will miss a crucial part of the Gospel. That verse we read together in Romans 5:8 used the phrase "while we were still sinners..." When trying to figure out how to relate with an audience, the goal is to figure out what their "while" is.

What sin is currently taking place in their life that God needs to meet them right in the middle of? That's what you want to hit on with your audience. To do that, you need to understand your audience. You have to be willing to meet people where they are and show them that God does the same. But how do you figure out where people are? I am glad you asked.

1. Assess personal struggles - People sometimes think that teachers and communicators of the Bible are fake. While in some cases that may be true, that doesn't mean we have to be. I want people to know that I am a real person with real struggles. In the words of Pastor Craig Groeschel, "People would rather follow a leader who is real than one who is always right." When you sit back and think of the struggles you have had in the past, it's an excellent opportunity for you to relate with people. It is also incredibly healing because it will bring purpose to the pain you have experienced in your life. People need to know that you are a real person and that God understands real issues. Here are a few questions to ask yourself:

What are my past struggles?

What are my current struggles?

2. Ask the opinions of others - This seems like it would be a no-brainer for us, but it isn't. Sometimes our pride kicks in, and we feel like we can just handle it on our own. If you are taking notes throughout this book, write this down: great leaders ask for insight. It's ok to openly admit that you don't know everything. I am a white guy who grew up in the bible belt, and it would be ignorant for me to think that I understand the struggles of an African-American male in the South. So rather than assuming or injecting a half-baked opinion, ask those who you are trying to reach. Don't be afraid to ask a high school student or single mom or homosexual their biggest struggle. If I can understand you better, I can show you that God meets you where you are, and that is the goal! Here are a few questions to ask yourself:

Is there someone who has a better perspective on this issue?

Am I consistently talking with people who are different than me?

3. Research topics - We have so much information at our fingertips! Pick up a book, read a blog, Google something. There is an infinite amount of resources that you and I have to learn about how people feel. Barna, a research company, is one of those incredible resources I use often. In a recent message, I was trying to get a good grasp on how millennials view their work. Barna research showed that millennials bring optimism and ambition into their workplace. Simple research gave me a new understanding and great sermon content! Here are a few questions to ask yourself:

Who has researched the audience I am trying to reach?

What sources am I looking into to better reach the people God has given me?

4. Pray for understanding - This is probably the most important one of these points. James 1:5 says, "If any of you lacks wisdom, you should ask God, who gives generously to all without finding fault, and it will be given to you." I think God is waiting in Heaven for you and me to tag Him in for fresh insight. After all, God cares way more for the people who you are communicating to than you do. Pray for your audience; ask God for ways to relate with the audience He has called you to minister to. As you start the process of message preparation, take some time and pray for your audience. Invite God to give you eyes to see past the current condition of people. Here is a prayer you can pray:

"God, I ask You to open my eyes to see these people the way You see them. Help me to see past the surface and connect with them. Not so that they like me more, but that they know You love them. Amen."

Cast A Wide Net

This feeling is unlike anything you have ever experienced before. It's this stomach-turning, palm-sweating, heart-racing feeling that you have as you sit on that front row. It may be during a video introduction of a new series or the in-person opening. Regardless, you are nervous. You clear your throat, walk out on to the stage, and you begin to deliver the word that God has placed on your heart.

I will never forget the first sermon I preached. I have the audio recording of it and listen back every once in a while when I need to be reminded of how good God's grace is. When I first started preaching and opening the scriptures with people, I didn't have some of the tools I am sharing with you in this chapter. I would rush straight into things, make a beeline for my main point, and hope that you could keep up. I hoped that you would catch some of my passion for what I was teaching you and possibly give your life to Jesus.

Was there anything wrong with that? Nope. I think I was working with the training that I had at the time. It wasn't until I started asking God to grow me as a communicator that I realized Jesus had an interesting way of kicking off His messages. One of the things He did was what I like to call "cast a wide net." Jesus had a way of grabbing the majority of an audience's attention and then delivered His message. Let me show you an example:

"He went on to tell the people this parable: "A man planted a vineyard, rented it to some farmers and went away for a long time." Luke 20:9 NIV

Jesus starts the opening of the message by giving us three scenes in one short verse. You can be sure of this, everything in scripture is intentional not accidental. When we read that, it may be easy just to skip over, but this is how Jesus captures the attention of His audience. Here are a few ways Jesus throws the net out wide for a big catch:

A man plants - Farming was a part of everyday life for the people in this time. It was the food supply and wine was the customary drink. When a man plants a vineyard there is food and drink on his table. People didn't have to conjure up some imaginative figure Jesus was talking about; they understood it because they lived it.

Working business owners - Next, Jesus mentions a group of farmers who rent the vineyard from the owner of the land. Even early in the Bible, there is an entrepreneurial spirit inside of people. This group of people would be pioneers in their efforts to farm land that is not their own.

Disappearing owner - And then, to make sure the net was cast wide enough, He tosses in the fact that the owner of the vineyard leaves for a very long time. Have you ever been hard at work and it seems like someone else just disappears? I have too.

These three things allowed Jesus to cast a wide net and helped Him relate to the people He was trying to reach. He tells a parable using characters so relatable to these people, they can't help but listen. I think one of the greatest ways to kick off a message is with an introduction that shows our audience that we understand them.

Every week people are coming into our churches, small groups, Sunday school classes, student ministries, etc., in one of three places. They are either going into a storm, in the middle of a storm or coming out of one. Regardless, people experience storms throughout life and need to know that God not only understands it, but gave us His Word to equip us to navigate rocky waters. People need you to help them see that God understands where they are and is ready to guide them out of it.

CONNECTION BEFORE CORRECTION

I was catching an early morning flight out of Charlotte. I am not an early morning person, and no amount of coffee fixes that. When I fly, there are a few things that are a must: over-ear headphones, phone, and some gummy worms. I made it through security and was waiting at my gate for boarding. The room was empty but I watched as someone came into the lobby who looked super eager to be flying today.

I try not to be judgmental of people but remember, it's like 6am. Yes I know, it being early morning is never an excuse to sin, but let's continue. I prayed hard that the Lord would graciously guide and direct this guy to sit somewhere far from me. But God has a sense of humor. That man, sure enough, sat right in front of me, eager to chat. My headphones were on which should have been the international symbol for "I have no desire to talk", but not for this guy. He smiled, leaned in, and began to eagerly tell me all about his upcoming trips.

Within the first few sentences I knew we were in different stages of life. He was eager and excited to tell me about the last time he went to this place, all the clubs, and all the women he slept with. I hate to even write this, but I wasn't filled with compassion for the guy, I just wanted out of the conversation. The announcement came over the intercom and I was able to board the plane. I thanked God for what I thought was His provision to get me out of that situation. You have probably see what's coming. Yes, his seat was right beside mine.

As he sat down, I felt the Lord say, "I brought him to you." I felt terrible. What I saw as an inconvenience or interruption to a morning flight was actually a divine opportunity. I took my headphones off and just listened to him chat for the next hour. I can't write a quarter of the things he said, but he poured his heart out. At the end of it, he said, "So tell me, what do you do for a living?" I pondered whether or not to lie, but decided honesty was the best route. I let him know that I was a pastor and I watched shame overcome him. He grew incredibly uncomfortable and started to shut down. So I asked him a follow-up question, "At this point in your life do you feel closer or further from God than before?" He said, "further," without any hesitation.

For the remainder of the plane ride, I had the opportunity to share my story with him. The relentless pursuit of God that rescued me from drug addiction and gave me purpose and fulfillment. The more we began to talk, the less shame and more joy he had. After sharing my struggles with him, he said, "You aren't like the Christians I know." I knew just the ones he was referring to. They were Christians who would have heard his story and immediately felt the need to tell him the 518 reasons why God didn't approve.

He had been around people who used scripture, not as a weapon against Satan, but a weapon against people. I think people land there whenever they miss out on a principle we see Jesus live out: connection before correction.

Jesus had a similar encounter to mine in John 4. A divine encounter that would lead to someone knowing that God meets you where you are.

> *"Jacob's well was there; and Jesus, tired from the long walk, sat wearily beside the well about noontime. Soon a Samaritan woman came to draw water, and Jesus said to her, "Please give me a drink." He was alone at the time because his disciples had gone into the village to buy some food. The woman was surprised, for Jews refuse to have anything to do with Samaritans. She said to Jesus, "You are a Jew, and I am a Samaritan woman. Why are you asking me for a drink?" Jesus replied, "If you only knew the gift God has for you and who you are speaking to, you would ask me, and I would give you living water.""*
> *John 4:6-10 NLT*

I love the humanity of Jesus that John reveals to us in scripture. Jesus had been walking for some time and needed a drink. So He sits down, and an unsuspecting individual walks up. It wasn't uncommon for women to come to draw water, but at the hottest part of the day? That was unheard of! It's almost like God wanted you and me to know that when we least expect to encounter Him, He is right there waiting. She is astonished because men didn't interact with women like this. Also, Jews and Samaritans didn't associate like this, which left her starstruck. Jesus met her right in the middle of her mess, and He knew that she was avoiding something, but that didn't stop Him. After some chit-chat about water and a bucket, Jesus says this:

"Anyone who drinks this water will soon become thirsty again. But those who drink the water I give will never be thirsty again. It becomes a fresh, bubbling spring within them, giving them eternal life." "Please, sir," the woman said, "give me this water! Then I'll never be thirsty again, and I won't have to come here to get water." "Go and get your husband," Jesus told her. "I don't have a husband," the woman replied. Jesus said, "You're right! You don't have a husband— for you have had five husbands, and you aren't even married to the man you're living with now. You certainly spoke the truth!"" John 4:13-18 NLT

Did you see it? Jesus didn't start with, "Hey, you have been sleeping around with a few guys, and the one you are shacked up with now isn't your husband." He started by sitting down with her, strategically positioned to show God's love. The connection was in the heart of God way before correction ever took place. We see the entire conversation play out with Jesus and this woman. He knew about her relationship issues when they began the conversation. Yet, He chose to participate in small talk and reveal that there was more to life than what she was currently experiencing.

I believe that no matter the format or length message you are preparing to deliver, God wants you to sit on the edge of a well to communicate with someone who is far from Him. Much like that woman at the well, God wants each person to know that He will do whatever it takes to meet people where they are. I remember the moment when I got a glimpse of God's pursuit for me, it was life-changing. At the same time, I eagerly await the opportunity to share that truth with others!

"CONNECTION WAS ON THE HEART OF GOD BEFORE CORRECTION EVER TOOK PLACE.

CHAPTER FIVE

WHERE GOD WANTS YOU TO BE (VISION)

"When I think of vision, I have in mind the ability to see above and beyond the majority."
- Chuck Swindoll

"And the Lord answered me: 'Write the vision; make it plain on tablets, so he may run who reads it.'"
- Habakkuk 2:2 ESV

Did you know that 47% of Americans wear glasses? If you go to fact-check that, you won't find it because I made it up. However, over the last few years, I have joined whatever percentage there is of those who wear glasses. I haven't always worn glasses, but while teaching one Sunday morning, I noticed my Bible was getting harder and harder to read. If you can smell the pages of your Bible, it may be too close to your face.

I was reluctant to get my eyes checked because I hate doctors and just lumped optometrists in with that. With a few kicks and a shove, my wife got me to go in for an exam. During which, the doctor jokingly said, "You drove here without glasses?" Followed by, "You'd be better off without a right eye." How encouraging is that? I knew he was right, though. From the inability to read things far and close and the occasional running into things, I realized I had a vision problem.

About a week passed and I received my glasses in the mail. They came in a box and a fancy little case I would never use again. I removed the plastic and put them on. As they rested on the bridge of my nose, the spirit of Aladdin came upon me, and I began to sing, "A whole new world, a new fantastic point of view!" Maybe a little overdramatic, but it was amazing. My eyes were opened to new wonders and possibilities because I could finally see! Here is what scripture says about vision:

"If people can't see what God is doing, they stumble all over themselves; But when they attend to what he reveals, they are most blessed." Proverbs 29:18 MSG

I think as a society, we have a vision problem. The King James Version of Proverbs 29:18 says, "The people perish." Doesn't that sound like the condition of our world currently? People are perishing and stumbling all over themselves because they can't see what God is doing. I think that it's our job as communicators to help people regain vision. This chapter is designed to help increase your capacity to see what God sees. Once you have vision to see, you can feel more equipped to share His perfect plan for the rest of the world!

ALPHA AND OMEGA

December 6, 2010 is one of those days I tend to think back to on occasion. It was the day before my birthday, and I had gone into the doctor to find out the results of some blood work that was taken. The doctor walked in and asked if I wanted the good news or bad news first. My heart fell into the pit of my stomach and time slowed down. That moment felt like an eternity, even though it was just a few seconds long. He began to tell me that I had Graves Disease. All I knew was that a grave is what you go into when you die. The bad news was that we didn't catch it early and it was causing my resting heart rate to live around 120 bpm. At any moment, my heart could explode.

We talked through the options and he placed me on medication, but I left that day with minimal hope of survival. This thing had the potential to end my life. You are reading this book now, so as you may have guessed, I made it. Ha! Take that Graves Disease! You lost and I won my life (and a mountain of medical bills). One of the things I look back on and realize now, is that had I known the outcome of what was going to take place, I would have responded differently. Unlike God, I do not see the beginning and the end.

"I am the Alpha and the Omega, the First and the Last, the Beginning and the End." Revelation 22:13 NLT

The name "Alpha and Omega" means beginning and end. Oh how we love repetition. That verse says, "I am the Beginning and the End, the First and the Last, the Beginning and the End." I think God wanted you and me to know a few things about

Him; things that are crucial to understanding how He sees things.

1. He sees the full timeline - Often, when I find myself frustrated with God, it is because we see things differently. God and I have a different vantage point. I see things right in front of me in the here and now, while God has a 30,000-foot view of my entire life. He sees the decisions I am making now, knowing how they play a role in my outcome. Part of understanding God's vision is realizing that He has the full picture while you and I have a snapshot. God sees your beginning, He sees your end, and desires to guide and direct your steps to His preferred future for your life. Isaiah 46:10 says that God is "declaring the end from the beginning," not the other way around. Trust that when God began with you, the end was in mind, and He plans to prosper, not harm you (Jeremiah 29:11).

2. He finishes what He starts - Can I come to you for a moment of confession? I have a big problem in my life. I have a habit of starting things and never finishing them. There are so many DIY projects that I started with such passion, only for it to fade into the background when something else came along. Philippians 1:6 says, "Being confident of this, that He who began a good work in you will carry it on to completion until the day of Christ Jesus." We serve a faithful God who can be trusted to finish what He began! Paul assures us that we can be confident about that very thing. Life, situations, and circumstances may say that God is finished. Make no mistake, He is the same yesterday, today, and forever (Hebrews 13:8). He hasn't stopped finishing what He started in the past, and He won't start now.

When you are preaching God's word to people, they are often stuck in today, paralyzed by the overwhelming weight of the here and now. Be sure to let them in on the fact that God has a beginning-to-end vision for their life. No moment is a surprise to Him! Communicate in a way that allows people to tap into God's aerial view of their life. If God sees it, I think He wants us to see it as well.

PAST PROBLEMS

My heart goes out to people who are stuck in drug addiction. I feel for them because I was once one of them. Drug use is not just a problem anymore, it's an epidemic that is killing almost 100,000 people a year. My heart breaks when Christians look at people with drug addictions and judge them rather than help them. When you look at someone who is broken and hurting, if your response isn't compassion, you don't see as God sees. God's vision can see past their current condition and into His preferred future for their life. God looks past the outward appearance of issues and into the heart. He sees the person behind a problem, and God loves people!

In John 5, we see a disabled man at the pool of Bethesda. The word on the street was if you were the first one to get into the water after an angel stirred it up, you would be healed. Naturally, sick and broken people want to be healed, so they flocked to this pool. Hundreds of people were scattered in this area in the hope of experiencing the healing power of God. Jesus enters the scene, and God highlights someone to Him, a man in need of a touch from God.

"When Jesus saw him lying there, and knew that he already had been in that condition a long time, He said to him, "Do you want to be made well?"" John 5:6 NKJV

Pause with me for a moment on that verse. Jesus **saw** his condition, but **chose** to ask the guy if he wanted to get better. Was Jesus insensitive or cold-hearted? No. He saw past the problem and current situation of the individual and tapped into his humanity. He looked past the problem that the man had and talked to the person. He didn't talk down to the guy who was broken, but met him where he was.

Being Jesus, He would have known precisely what the man needed, but rather than just doing it, He struck up a conversation. He didn't talk down to the man with problems; He talked to the man with problems. I would implore you as a communicator to not talk down to broken and hurting people, because we are no better than they are. Let us dive back into the text and see the man's response to Jesus:

> *"The sick man answered Him, "Sir, I have no man to put me into the pool when the water is stirred up; but while I am coming, another steps down before me." Jesus said to him, "Rise, take up your bed and walk." And immediately the man was made well, took up his bed, and walked."*
> *John 5:7-9 NKJV*

Have you ever had a conversation with someone only to have no idea who they were? That is this guy's story. With no recognition of who Jesus is, he needs someone to put him into the pool so that he could be healed. Jesus wasn't offended that He wasn't recognized; He jumped into action. "You want to be healed?" Jesus asked. "Get up and start walking." A miracle happened right there before their eyes! Jesus had healed the man of a condition that had plagued him for years.

"GOD SEES THE PERSON BEHIND THE PROBLEM, AND GOD LOVES PEOPLE.

I believe that to see like Jesus we have to look past the current condition of people, focusing on the restored version of them. I think that when Jesus walked up to the broken man laying on a mat, He saw past the brokenness. Jesus saw a man that, through His power, could experience things that he never thought possible. He could experience healing, restoration, and the grace of God in a new way. This is an isolated event for this man, but I think it is God's viewpoint for all broken and hurting people. When God looks at you, He sees where you could be in Him!

Remember that the current condition of a drug

addict can change by merely having an encounter with Jesus. I am living proof that, with Christ, drug addicts can become pastors and teachers of God's Word. I am so thankful that God saw past my current condition!

CAKE BAKING

My wife loves baking cakes and I consider myself the official taste-tester of our home. Baking a cake isn't for the faint of heart. There is a list of ingredients and step-by-step instructions to achieve the perfect dessert. If you take that list of ingredients and alter them in any way, you change the outcome. Have you ever wondered what God wants your life to look like on this earth? What "ingredients" would be listed in His recipe? The Apostle Paul writes to us in Galatians 5 to give us an insight on just that:

"The acts of the flesh are obvious: sexual immorality, impurity and debauchery; idolatry and witchcraft; hatred, discord, jealousy, fits of rage, selfish ambition, dissensions, factions and envy; drunkenness, orgies, and the like. I warn you, as I did before, that those who live like this will not inherit the kingdom of God. But the fruit of the Spirit is love, joy, peace, [patience], kindness, goodness, faithfulness, gentleness and self-control. Against such things there is no law." Galatians 5:19-23 NIV

Did you catch what Paul is doing? He is acknowledging where the people currently are because ignoring it doesn't fix anything. When you choose to recognize where you are, you can better see the contrast of where God wants you to be. Paul shows us that God has a recipe for your life in Christ. This recipe has an ingredient list of nine things that change the results you see in your life. I want to go through each of the nine fruits of the Spirit and help us see God's preferred future. Having these nine fruits active and vibrant in our lives is the only way to end up where God wants us to be.

As a communicator, I believe that it is our job to give these ingredients to our people. Don't carry the pressure of having to come up with the perfect recipe, God gave us one! We simply get to bake with His recipe using His ingredients and I can promise that the outcome is incredible. Let's take a look at each ingredient below:

Love - The first fruit of the Spirit is love. As cliché as it may sound, typically we love "love". It is something that we check off the list quickly because we feel like we already understand it. I would propose to you that God desires for your life to be marked by love because if it isn't, your life is not marked by God.

"Whoever does not love does not know God, because God is love." 1 John 4:8 NIV

You and I will never be in the position to give away that which we have not yet received. Maybe you have tried to love others but you find yourself tired and frustrated from it. I would suggest to you that you will only give love to the measure which you have allowed God to love you. It was the love of God that pursued us when we had turned our backs on Him. It was the love of God that sent Jesus to earth to live a sinless life and suffer for us. It was God's love for the world that Jesus remained on the cross to die, though He could have saved Himself at any moment. When we understand the love that God has for us, our capacity to love others is expanded. I believe the ingredient of love must be experienced and then extended to a lost and broken world.

Joy - When we say we want joy in our lives what most of imagine is something much like, or the same as, happiness. However, joy and happiness don't come from the same source. Happiness is an emotional reaction to a circumstance or situation, while joy is a gift given by God. Joy surpasses your circumstances and is not rooted in anything other than your relationship with God.

"Consider it pure joy, my brothers and sisters, whenever you face trials of many kinds, because you know that the testing of your faith produces perseverance."
James 1:2-3 NIV

You may be thinking, "How can I have pure joy in the middle of suffering?" For those of us who call ourselves followers of Jesus, joy is a complete delight in God. The source of our joy is Jesus, and our source doesn't change based on situations. Let me say it louder for the people in the back. Pure joy is complete delight in God, even when all hell is breaking loose in your life. I believe God wants you to have that joy today, no matter where you currently are. Don't feel like you have that? Neither did David. In Psalm 51, David asks that the Lord would "restore the joy of his salvation." If you have lost your joy, it may sound simple, but ask God to restore it. He is a good heavenly Father who loves to lavish His children with gifts (Matthew 7:11).

Peace - We live in a world of continual conflict and that isn't going to change anytime soon. The storms of life will come raging in at some point in your life, and when they do I think you can take a stance that changes everything. In God's preferred future for you and me, there is an opportunity to rise above the conflict you will inevitably face. Peace is not the absence of storms, it is a posture in the middle of it.

"Then he got into the boat and his disciples followed him. Suddenly a furious storm came up on the lake, so that the waves swept over the boat. But Jesus was sleeping."
Matthew 8:23-24 NLT

How in the world could Jesus be sleeping while the other disciples were panicking? Ono word, peace. One of the names that Jesus is given is the "Prince of Peace" (Isaiah 9:6). Peace is not something that Jesus obtained, it's who He is! Since you and I are in a relationship with God, we have access to that same peace (John 16:33). In Christ, you have the ability to take the world's greatest nap in life's most chaotic storm. To access that peace, lean into the source of peace Himself, Jesus Christ. That peace that only comes from Christ will transcend all human comprehension and guard your heart and mind when things get tough (Philippians 4:7).

Patience - One of the worst things you can pray for in life is patience, because God will give you 1,000 opportunities to develop it. I am not a very patient person, but I have learned that patience isn't my issue . My problem is that sometimes I don't trust that God's timing is better than mine. Much like in cake baking, in life there are some ingredients that have to be added at just the right time. Let me ask you this, do you believe that God's timing is better than your own? Perhaps, through scripture, we can see that God has us completely covered.

"But at just the [right time], God sent his Son, born of a woman, subject to the law." Galatians 4:4 NIV

At just the right time, Jesus was sent to the world to be born of a woman. Take hope in this, we serve a God who knows when to start something. If it hasn't started, it isn't time for it yet. Maybe it hasn't started in your life because God isn't done preparing you for what He wants to start.

"When we were utterly helpless, Christ came at just the right time and died for us sinners." Romans 5:6 NLT

It wasn't a fluke or a coincidence that "at just the right time" Christ died for you and me! It was just that, the right time. We serve a God who has our current situation covered just as much as He knows when things should start. Trusting in the timing of God is knowing that He isn't surprised by what we're currently facing, and He isn't jumping ship in the rough times.

"And I am certain that God, who began the good work within you, will continue his work until it is finally finished on the day when Christ Jesus returns." Philippians 1:6 NLT

Remember, God isn't giving up on you! He isn't finished with you and is going to continue the work that He began. We serve a God who is faithful to complete what He starts. Trusting in God's timing is knowing that He knows when to start things, has your current situation covered, and will see things through to the end. When you believe that, patience is simply a by-product of trusting in God's sovereignty.

Kindness - When I was in kindergarten, I came home one day and told my grandma about this mean, rude, demon-possessed kid who pushed me down and called me names. She smiled and stared straight through my little soul as grandmas can, and gave me this advice, "Kill them with kindness." God and my grandma knew something that it took me years to understand. Kindness is the delivery mechanism for the grace of God. Look at what scripture says about kindness:

"God's kindness leads you toward repentance."
Romans 2:4 NLT

It isn't great preaching, a bible study, or a 12-step program that leads broken people to turn from their ways. It is the kindness of God in us, extended from one undeserving individual to another, that leads people toward repentance. It is the kindness of God that can soften even the hardest of hearts. Communicator of the Gospel, don't miss this fruit of the Spirit. If you do, you will have people who turn to God out of duty rather than delight. God will become a dictator who rules over us rather than a kind, life-giving Father who desires a relationship with us.

Goodness - When we read the list of fruits, I always forget this one. Truthfully, in the editing of this book it was revealed that I had left it out. I sat back and wondered if perhaps I didn't find this ingredient necessary, but that wasn't it. The fruit of goodness is one that I believe just comes naturally when you live like Jesus. You aren't doing good things so that Jesus will love you, you love Jesus and in return you do good things.

"...how God anointed Jesus of Nazareth with the Holy Spirit and power, and how he went around doing good and healing all who were under the power of the devil, because God was with him." Acts 10:38 NIV

Jesus was filled with the Spirit and because of that, He did good things. Following Jesus should move us into action to do good things for the world around us. This ingredient in your cake may need to be stirred in with a little elbow grease to make sure it becomes a part of you. There is nothing more useless than a person who claims to know Jesus but does nothing with it.

Gentleness - I've always found it strange that kindness and gentleness are both on the list. They are so similar yet so different at the same time. Kindness is the external expression of the internal heart posture of God (gentleness). Another word for gentleness in the Bible is tenderheartedness. I believe that God wants us to be tenderhearted. A hard heart will hoard the blessing and goodness of God for itself, but a tender heart will give away what it has received.

> *"Be kind to one another, tenderhearted, forgiving*
> *one another, as God in Christ forgave you."*
> *Ephesians 4:32 NLT*

Being gentle is not a sign of weakness but rather of strength. We live in a cold and dark world where becoming hard-hearted is incredibly easy. We must allow God to transform our hearts to become tender towards others. Allow God to keep your heart tender or you may become bitter and angry (Ephesians 4:31).

Faithfulness- The fruit of faithfulness has a companion by the name of perseverance. They are time-tested brothers in arms in the spiritual battle that you and I will face in our walk with Christ. Faithfulness is what allows us to push through the hard times, remembering that we are not here by accident. God has marked, called, chosen, and appointed you, and by continuing to move, you win! In the words of Dory from Finding Nemo, "Just keep swimming."

"Blessed is the one who perseveres under trial because, having stood the test, that person will receive the crown of life that the Lord has promised to those who love him." James 1:12 NLT

Faithfulness is the very thing that keeps your feet moving when you feel like the enemy has tried to get you to stop. The fruit of faithfulness is the commitment to keep walking when you feel like giving up. That decision to keep moving will lead you to blessings that you could never have imagined! Your faithfulness will be tested, but faith that isn't tested is faith that cannot be trusted.

Self Control- I have often heard the expression used "save the best for last" and I think it's fitting here. While God does not have a ranking system for these fruits, this is my personal favorite of them all. I like it so much because I desire it the most. Having a drug-addicted life before Christ, I know what it is like to not have self-control. I was a slave to my sin, desires, and cravings. The easy thing to do would be to work hard and do better but that isn't part of God's recipe:

"Therefore, brothers and sisters, we have an obligation to do what our sinful nature desires. For if you live according to the desires of the flesh, you will die; but if by the Spirit you put to death the misdeeds of the body, you will live." Romans 8:12-13 NLT

The chains and shackles of obligation to sin have been broken off of your life. Every single time you get up to teach God's word, don't skip over the entanglement of sin. Address it head-on and proclaim this truth to anyone that will listen: if you are stuck in your sin, fighting won't fix it but surrendering to God will change everything. The moment you surrender to God, sin is no longer something you have to do, it's now a choice. Will you settle for the temporary fulfillment of the desire of your flesh or allow the Spirit of God to become your desire and source of fulfillment?

No matter who you are or where you are as a communicator of the Gospel, I would implore you to share these ingredients with your people. Grab your chef's hat and apron and start mixing in love, joy, peace, patience, kindness, goodness, gentleness, faithfulness, and self-control. It is ok to lean heavier on one ingredient for an individual message, but your people will need to hear about all nine at some point. Leaving out one of these ingredients will leave people with an unfinished, poor tasting cake.

LAST BREATH

I almost ended the chapter after that previous section but felt let by the Spirit to add this closing thought. It may mean nothing to you, or it may be the very reason God led you to pick up this book. I want you to know today that if you're not dead, God's not done in your life! When you are finished with your time here on earth, you will pass on and stand before God. For now, though, God still has purpose coursing through every fiber of your being. Your best days in Him are still in front of you!

"Then, even if your beginnings were modest, your final days will be full of prosperity." Job 8:7 CSB

In this moment, God wants you to realize that He is the God of new beginnings. You need one, I need one, and so do the people we communicate to. Maybe you feel like too many things have gone wrong in your life and you're disqualified from speaking. That is not how God works. His stamp of qualification is His Spirit. Perhaps you feel like you are too young or too old. You are never too young or too old to make a difference in the Kingdom of God.

Your start may not have been great, but this very moment is the perfect time to start fresh. You don't even have to wait for tomorrow or some big super-natural movement. As an old Chinese proverb says, "The best time to plant a tree is twenty years ago, but the second-best time is right now." My prayer for you is that as you read this right now, God is filling you with purpose and passion to go all out for Him until your last breath.

YOU ARE NEVER TOO YOUNG OR TOO OLD TO MAKE A DIFFERENCE IN THE KINGDOM OF GOD.

CHAPTER SIX

PLANKS
(POINTS AND APPLICATION)

"Growth is the only evidence of life."
- John Henry Newman

"being confident of this, that he who began a good
work in you will carry it on to completion until
the day of Christ Jesus."
- Philippians 1:6 NIV

I have a love-hate relationship with Pinterest. If you aren't familiar with Pinterest it is a social network that allows users to visually share and discover new interests by posting images or videos to their own or others' boards. If you are looking for the perfect dessert for that dinner party you are hosting? No problem, Pinterest has you covered. Want to take up DIY projects? The possibilities are endless. Are you looking for a Crossfit workout? Don't. Treat yourself to a donut and remind yourself that the cross is your fitness. With Pinterest, you can see the outcome of so many different "pins." Click on the image, and it opens up to a plethora of information, a "how-to" guide of sorts. As we were getting into our first set of offices at Propel, Pinterest became my best friend. We spent way too much time together. I had picked out colors, textures, and design aesthetic, all from the convenience of my phone.

There were large openings that I thought were perfect for barn doors and what I saw online was only confirming it. I needed three doors and found them for around $700 per door but with my budget, I couldn't afford one. Thankfully, Pinterest gave me a how-to guide on how to build barn doors. Had I ever built a door? Nope. But with someone guiding me through the process, I was able to do it with minimal mistakes!

I think that, deep down, people want to grow in their relationship with God, but don't know how. They want to surrender that sin issue, but don't know where to begin. They know their current friends aren't the best, but they don't know how to start making new ones. Your teaching needs to connect with them in a way that equips them to grow closer to God by taking one step at a time. In this chapter, we will talk about the importance of applying God's Word to people's everyday life and how sermon points reinforce what you are teaching them.

TEACH ME HOW

Do you remember learning to ride a bike? If you don't know how to ride a bike at this point in your life, there is still hope! There are plenty of videos online that will teach you how in a short period of time. (While you are watching videos, be sure to watch bike riding fails, they are in the top 10 of fail videos I enjoy). Learning to ride a bike for me was a process, as I am sure it was for you. It started with my dad buying me a bike with training wheels. This incredibly helpful tool attaches to the rear frame of the bike, creating stability. Without training wheels, you can easily tip over or fall because you don't know how to balance correctly. Luckily, we live in a world where training wheels have been invented.

As communicators it is easy to forget the role we play in people's lives. We forget that people don't know how to follow Christ wholeheartedly. Heck, there are times in my own life where I don't even know if I'm doing it right. When you and I teach God's Word with simple application and practical next steps, we allow people to have training wheels on. There is no shame in the training wheels because, had I not learned how to balance, I would never have learned to ride a bike. Perhaps the reason we have so many Christians today who profess Christ as Lord, but don't live like it, is because they never had someone teach them how to balance. If I can help you learn what it means to consistently feed your spirit and grow in your relationship with God, following Jesus doesn't become easier, it becomes the only outcome you desire.

When I think of someone who was an incredible guide for people, I think of Jesus. No one has ever been a better teacher than the one who is fully God and fully man. His humanity, coupled with His divinity, made Him the GOAT (greatest of all time). Jesus had a group of 12 men who looked up to Him and sought His input on things. When they didn't understand something, they ran to Jesus and asked Him for advice.

"One day Jesus was praying in a certain place. When He finished, one of His disciples said to Him, "Lord, teach us to pray..."" Luke 11:1 NIV

They couldn't figure out how this whole prayer thing worked and I can't blame them. I have felt the same way many times, as I am sure that you have too. So Jesus, being the Good Teacher, leans in and shows them a prayer:

"Our Father in Heaven, hallowed be Your Name. Your Kingdom come. Your will be done on earth as it is in Heaven. Give us this day our daily bread. And forgive us our debts, as we forgive our debtors. And do not lead us into temptation, but deliver us from the evil one. For Yours is the Kingdom and the power and the glory forever. Amen." Matthew 6:9-13 NKJV

Jesus was a spiritual tour guide for these men, and they listened to the words He had to say because they knew it would get them closer to God. I think you can see where I am going here; people are doing the exact same thing with you! They are looking to you, hanging on to the words that you have to say, in hopes that, through your words, they might grow closer to God. I believe, based on what we see Jesus do, a good spiritual guide does a few things:

1. They focus on God - Did you catch how Jesus starts the prayer off for His disciples in Matthew 6? First, remember that we are praying to **_"Our Father."_** Jesus was incredibly intentional about making sure that they focused on the right person. Then He says, "in Heaven, hallowed be Your name." It's all God-focused. He sets them on the reality of eternity so that they have the right focus. A good spiritual guide is one that shifts your focus and attention to God.

> _"The bride belongs to the bridegroom. The friend who attends the bridegroom waits and listens for him, and is full of joy when he hears the bridegroom's voice. That joy is mine, and it is now complete." John 3:29 NIV_

May we always remember who the bride (the body of Christ, the Church) belongs to. We are the friend, not the bridegroom. Our joy comes from seeing God's people encounter Him!

"A GOOD SPIRITUAL GUIDE IS ONE THAT SHIFTS YOUR FOCUS AND ATTENTION TO GOD.

2. They give instructions - When people have the desire to grow or change but don't know how, the best thing that they can receive is instruction. The simple act of giving them instructions can position them to receive something incredible from God. Matthew 6:9 starts with Jesus saying, "Pray like this." It wasn't a question, but rather a statement that was filled with Kingdom authority. This isn't the only time we see Jesus give instructions, we see it all throughout the Bible.

"And he directed the people to sit down on the grass. Taking the five loaves and the two fish and looking up to heaven, he gave thanks and broke the loaves. Then he gave them to the disciples, and the disciples gave them to the people." Matthew 14:19 NIV

Jesus asked the people to sit and the disciples to serve. As they started handing things out, a few pieces of bread and some fish turned into more than enough to feed 5,000. God has instilled boldness inside of you and given you authority to teach His Word. Don't abuse that authority, but rather use it to help people. Instruct them and help them get into position to experience the power of God at work.

3. They create patterns to follow - If you want to be a good spiritual guide, you must get used to creating patterns for other people to follow. You will develop patterns for yourself and patterns for people to follow. As a communicator of the Gospel, people are watching your steps and looking at how you do things. You are modeling for them what it looks like to follow Christ. It is a part of your calling that you must embrace, as Paul did:

"Follow my example, as I follow the example of Christ." 1 Corinthians 11:1 NLT

You are paving the way for people and they will follow you as you follow Christ. Jesus led by example in this by giving the disciples an outline for how to pray. Be sure you create a path for people to follow.

A. CONNECT WITH GOD RELATIONALLY
"Our Father in Heaven."

B. WORSHIP HIS NAME
"Hallowed be Your Name."

C. PRAY HIS AGENDA FIRST
"Your Kingdom come. Your will be done on earth as it is in Heaven."

D. DEPEND ON HIM FOR EVERYTHING
"Give us this day our daily bread."

E. FORGIVE AND BE FORGIVEN
"Forgive us our debts, as we forgive our debtors."

F. ENGAGE IN SPIRITUAL WARFARE
"And do not lead us into temptation, but deliver us from the evil one."

G. EXPRESS FAITH IN GOD'S ABILITY
"For Yours is the Kingdom and the power and the glory forever."

INFORMATION OVERLOAD

As I write this sentence, I have four different devices active. I have my laptop, my cell phone, a desktop computer, and my iPad. Not to mention, I also have my Bible, a study Bible, one spiritual growth book, and a leadership book on my desk. At my fingertips is a wealth of information. We live in a world where it is easier than ever to have access to the things we want to know. When you have access to this much information, though, it seems that most things just become white noise.

I think we have multiple generations of people who live in information overload. There are so many streams of information that we can't decide what to start on. So inevitably, we don't start at all. Information alone isn't going to cut it in your walk with God, it's what you do with that information that changes you from the inside out. I think many people who are new to the faith fall into the trap of believing that the equation below is the way things work.

Information = Transformation

It seems like this would work, right? It sure would be a lot simpler if this were the case. The Kingdom of God would increase in numbers so quickly because all people would need to do to be transformed is hear information. That would also mean that you and I would no longer have to say yes to Jesus, we would just have to hear about Him. You have all the information so transformation just happens. I know sarcasm doesn't always translate well in written form, but I do hope you are picking up what I'm putting down. Information alone will never be enough to overcome sin's entanglement in our lives.

"But be doers of the word, and not hearers only, deceiving yourselves." James 1:22 NKJV

Hearing alone will lead us down a path of deception. I can't speak for you, but I do know that personally, I don't want to live deceived. My desire is that those I teach don't live deceived either. There is a missing component to the thought process of the first equation: application. This is where you and I put our money where our mouth is. Application shows whether or not we believe what we say we do. I believe the outcome of transformation is made up of two things.

Information + Application = Transformation

Having all of the information is not enough to get you to the place of transformation. I can have the knowledge and desire to lose weight and get in shape, but if I never put the donuts down and pick up a gym membership, it isn't happening. The same is true with God's word; we must take action after reading it to experience transformation.

"Therefore, I urge you, brothers and sisters, in view of God's mercy, to offer your bodies as a living sacrifice, holy and pleasing to God—this is your true and proper worship. Do not copy the behavior and customs of this world, but let God transform you into a new person by changing the way you think. Then you will learn to know God's will for you, which is good and pleasing and perfect."
Romans 12:1-2 NIV

Paul invites us into a new way of living and doing things, but it only happens after we take the action of presenting our bodies as a living sacrifice to God (v1). Through that act of surrender, God transforms you into a new person, starting with the renewal of your mind. It's the action step toward God that leads us to transformation!

I believe our responsibility as communicators of the Gospel is to help people take those action steps. From a practical perspective, when you are preparing your message, remember that without the application of God's Word, people will just receive information from you. I desire that people leave understanding how to take action steps with what they have been taught that morning. It only takes one step for them to become closer to God, which is what we want.

I know far too many pastors who develop informational talks for their people. Information is good, but application is far greater than just filling a 45-minute time slot with content. If what people hear on Sunday doesn't cause them to take action on Monday, then Sunday didn't matter. I don't need people to sit and just listen to what I have to say every week, I need them to do something. We want them to exit the doors of our churches ready to make changes that shift their relationship with God and impact the lives of the world around them. Light always shines best in darkness and our job as communicators is to ensure that people know how to keep their flame lit and growing. Then the world will see their good deeds and glorify our Father in Heaven (Matthew 5:14-16).

K.I.S.S.

In the 1960s, the US Navy coined an acronym that I have come to appreciate over the years. It uses the word "kiss," which stands for "keep it simple, stupid." It seems a little bit demeaning, but I think that the thought process behind it is spot on. The truth is, it's sometimes easier for you and I to make it complicated. Simple isn't easy because it simply seems too good to be true. The Gospel has, will, and will forever be too good to be true. Perhaps you and I can shift the statement to "keep it stupid simple" as a reminder to do just that, keep it simple. It is in the simplicity of your message points and application that your listeners can run with what you have taught them.

"And the LORD answered me: "Write the vision; make it plain on tablets, so he may run who reads it.""
Habakkuk 2:2 NLT

The Lord gave Habakkuk a word and it was time to deliver it to the people. So, God instructs him to write it out and make it plain. Translation: "Hey, you better communicate this in a way that is simple because if you don't, people won't do anything with it." Sermon points that aren't simple lead to immobilized people. However, sermon points that are simple allow people to run with it. Where do they run, you might ask? They go right into the darkest corners of the world carrying the brightest light of them all. So friend, keep it stupid simple. Lost people who have never heard about Jesus are depending on it.

As we wrap up our time together in this chapter, I wanted to end on a practical note. If you picked up this book for the practical message prep stuff, it's coming. However, if you don't have a good foundation or understanding of the "bridge the gap" concept, it won't work. Right now, we are collecting puzzle pieces and the picture will soon unfold. Here are four tips for creating and writing simple points/ application steps in your messages:

1. Must be biblically accurate - If it doesn't line up with scripture, it doesn't belong in your message. False teaching is not something that I think you want to fall into. Make sure that when you approach scripture, you let scripture formulate your opinions. If you try and make scripture fit your opinions, you will twist and manipulate the very words of God to promote your agenda.

2. Make it relatable - People don't care how much you know until they know how much you care. Take the time to ensure that, even in your points, you are meeting them where they are. Relate with them on a personal level and invite them to take real next steps. I often like to use words like "we" instead of "you" so that the listener knows I am not excusing myself from what I am asking them to do.

3. Make them memorable - This is the most common advice you receive in communicating. It is true, though, if you can make it memorable it will be easier for people to carry it into the world. It may be something culturally relevant, a rhyme scheme, an acronym, or words that start with the same letter. Find whatever makes it memorable and go with it.

4. Keep them short, If possible - Just because you have an idea doesn't mean you have a good sermon point. Every point needs to go through a refinement process to ensure that it is being communicated in it's purest form. Keeping things under ten words is my goal for a sermon point.

"SERMON POINTS THAT AREN'T SIMPLE LEAD TO IMMOBILIZED PEOPLE.

CHAPTER SEVEN

ROPES
(JESUS)

"Afflictions are light when compared with what we really deserve. They are light when compared with the sufferings of the Lord Jesus. But perhaps their real lightness is best seen by comparing them with the weight of glory which is awaiting us..."
- A.W Pink

"The Word became a human being and, full of grace and truth, lived among us. We saw his glory, the glory which he received as the Father's only Son."
- John 1:14 NLT

I have been looking forward to writting this chapter since I started this book. I thought many times about starting the book with Jesus because I believe He more than deserves the number one slot. However, I have saved the chapter on Jesus for last in this section intentionally. I think that if you stacked up the messages of some churches in America, you would only have three of the four elements of the concept we have spoken about.

Relating with people, not too difficult. Seeing God's preferred future, I can totally do that. Give a few practical and helpful tips to you, no problem. For some people that's where they stop. So many people come into our churches only to be puffed up by self-help. That is not the message we should preach because that isn't God's message. Without Jesus none of this works. Jesus represents the ropes in our illustration because He holds it all together. Sounds good, but it's not even my idea. We see this concept all throughout God's Word.

"And he is before all things, and in him all things hold together." Colossians 1:17 NIV

Christ is the very thing that holds everything together. If you leave Him out, you will not be speaking on behalf of God. God does not have a message that exists outside of His Son, Jesus.

FOUNDATION

Our life experiences, circumstances, and situations shape and mold what we believe about everything. There are opinions that I have formulated based on the experiences I have had. For example, I believe, without a doubt, that baseball stadiums have the best hotdogs. Just like movie theaters have the best popcorn, even though you have to sell a kidney on the black market to afford it.

Whether good or bad, your experiences dictate the way you relate to God. If your earthly father walked out on you, there may be something looming in the back of your mind wondering when God will abandon you. Maybe you experienced church hurt. Therefore, all churches and pastors are bad. Our experiences dictate what we believe and here is the problem: the type of Christianity that we see today isn't what it was created to be. I have a strong desire to help us understand who Jesus is because if we don't get this right, nothing works.

"Together, we are his house, built on the foundation of the apostles and the prophets. And the cornerstone is Christ Jesus himself. We are carefully joined together in him, becoming a holy temple." Ephesians 2:20-21 NLT

Jesus is the foundation of it all, and if we don't get this right, we don't have a solid foundation. If you wonder why the global Church is divided, it's because Christ isn't the cornerstone. The reason why Christians debate on social media platforms, rather than share Jesus with their friends, is that our foundation isn't right. Paul describes the church as being "carefully joined together." When Jesus is our foundation we are not only in unity, but we are growing into all that God desires for us!

In this chapter, I am going to strip down everything you believe about Jesus. You may be a biblical scholar or a recent convert, but no matter where you see yourself on a spiritual level, humor me for the next few pages. Drop your preconceived notions and religious traditions and just soak up scripture. I want to give you three fundamental things you need to know and understand to have Christ as your foundation.

1. Jesus is the promised Savior - In order to understand that Jesus is our Savior, we have to know what we need to be saved from. When people are asked what they think they should be saved from, the common answer I get is "Hell." I think this is a by-product of generations before me asking, "If you died tonight, would you go to Heaven or Hell?" Is it wrong to ask this question? Absolutely not. The problem is, when Jesus becomes just your escape from Hell, you can never experience Heaven on Earth. Jesus came for the primary purpose of saving us from sin.

"For our sake he made him to be sin who knew no sin, so that in him we might become the righteousness of God."
2 Corinthians 5:21 ESV

He comes to save us from sin. That's the role of our Savior. But at what time did God make this covenant with us? I would propose, Genesis 3, back in the garden when sin enters into the picture. We went through this story a little in chapter three, but I wanted to pull a trick out of God's book and repeat some things. When God is going over what life looks like after the fall, we read this:

"Then the LORD God said to the serpent, "Because you have done this, you are cursed more than all animals, domestic and wild. You will crawl on your belly, groveling in the dust as long as you live. And I will cause hostility between you and the woman, and between your offspring and her offspring. He will strike your head, and you will bruise his heel."" Genesis 3:14-15 NLT

Verse 15 of Genesis 3 is all about Jesus. It says the seed of the serpent would bruise the heel of the seed of the woman. The serpent is Satan and the off-spring of the woman is Jesus. Confused about when the prophecy of bruising would have been fulfilled? Look no further than the cross. A bruise is a sign of a temporary moment of pain or affliction. I have had so many bruises in my life. When we first started Propel Church, I wasn't used to having a hitch on the back of my truck. Every Sunday for about six months, my shin and the trailer hitch kissed. The bruise was epic. On the cross, Satan bruised Jesus through His death.

The best part about a bruise is that it's just temporary. Bruising suggests something that was not ultimate or final. Though wounded, the damage done to Jesus was not final. He came back from the dead three days later! The resurrection of Jesus Christ was the ultimate crushing of the enemies head. When Satan is laughing, thinking he has won, remember that the resurrection is coming! God isn't done pointing to Jesus in Genesis 3.

"And the LORD God made clothing from animal skins for Adam and his wife." Genesis 3:21 NLT

Even though Adam and Eve did wrong God

chooses to make clothing for them. Has anyone ever done anything wrong to you? When I have been done wrong, I don't feel like giving gifts. When people do me wrong, I pray things like "May one million sand fleas make their abode in your armpit." I am, of course, kidding. But seriously, Adam and Eve did wrong and God shows them His generosity. That's the God we serve! A loving, gracious, second-chance, third-chance, infinite-chance God.

The first sacrifice we see in the Bible is in Genesis 3:21. For God to have skin from an animal, there had to be an animal. If the animal is now skinless, the animal has been killed. Not trying to get graphic with this point, but I do want you to see the connection. To cover their mistakes something had to die, ultimately pointing us to the fact that God allowed Jesus to be killed so that we might be covered.

"But God demonstrates his own love for us in this: While we were still sinners, Christ died for us. Since we have now been justified by his blood, how much more shall we be saved from God's wrath through him!" Romans 5:8-9 NIV

Let this sink in for a moment; God allowed Jesus, His only Son, to be killed so that your sins could be covered. It is only through His bloodshed that you are justified. When did God set this plan into motion?

From the moment we sinned. He promised Jesus to come, and through His bloodshed, the world was reconciled to God. The good news for us is that the Savior we have been promised has already come. So many in scripture were waiting for this Savior. But we aren't! Jesus came, died, and is now waiting for you and me to respond to Him.

> GOD ALLOWED JESUS, HIS ONLY SON, TO BE KILLED SO THAT YOUR SINS COULD BE COVERED.

2. Jesus is the full payment of sin - Anyone who knows me could tell you that I love to spend money on things. I especially don't have a problem buying shoes. Church planting has slowed down my purchases, but if the Lord lays it on your heart to bless me with a fresh pair of sneakers, I am a size 12.

One day I was going through a thrift shop and I saw an incredible pair of shoes. The heavens parted and a glowing beam came down to reveal that they were my size. I tried them on and they fit perfectly. I walked to the counter, head held high, until the cashier rang them up. She said, "That will be $684.32," to which I replied, "Get behind me, Satan." I made that last part up, but the truth is, I had no idea what those shoes cost. I think sometimes we fail to realize that sin has a cost.

"For the wages of sin is death, but the free gift of God is eternal life through Christ Jesus our Lord."
Romans 6:23 NLT

In every single one of our lives there is a debt created by sin, but this debt cannot be paid with money. The only thing that can pay this debt is death. So God did just that, He died in our place. The full payment of your sin and mine was covered through the death of Jesus on the cross. When you accept what Jesus did for you on the cross, God places a deposit into your account. Suddenly, your account has been credited and there is no longer a debt. Jesus covered your debt!

Somtimes I find myself trying to pay for my sin myself. At times, I feel like if I work hard enough, live well enough, and do enough good things, I will be able to cover my debt. After all, do I even deserve to have my debt covered by God? The answer is no. But thankfully, God doesn't give us what we deserve. In the book of Galatians, Paul is talking to a group of people who are stuck trying to work for the gift God has given them. Here is what he says:

"I do not treat the grace of God as meaningless. For if keeping the law could make us right with God, then there was no need for Christ to die." Galatians 2:21 NLT

You and I should go ahead and resolve in our hearts that we will never be good enough to cover our sin. If we could, Paul says that there would have been no reason for Jesus to die. It's like someone walking up, handing you the keys to a brand new Bugatti La Voiture Noire priced at $12.5 Million, and saying, "This is my gift to you because I love you." While you are thankful for the kind gesture, you respond by saying, "I would like to pay for it or maybe work for it. Could I do something to earn it?" That situational thought process seems irrational. So why do we do that in our relationship with God?

If we could pay for our sin ourselves, He wouldn't have needed to die. But because we had sin, Christ came, lived a sinless life, and died in our place. On the cross, He cries out, "It is finished." Your debt has been covered. It's not a partial payment or down payment on your debt to which He will hopefully come back and finish paying later. It has been fully paid by believing in Jesus as your Lord and Savior. When God looks at you, He no longer sees you; He sees Christ in you and you are justified. It's just as if you never sinned. Why? Because the payment of Jesus was full, your debt was covered. You don't have to work for it when you can rest in it.

3. Jesus is our access to God - This is a foundational component to the truth of what scripture teaches us. Sin creates the gap between God and us, so we need a bridge, a gate, an entryway to have access to God. I remember back in my pre-Jesus days I would go to the bar with some of my friends. One night we were trying out a new bar downtown, but as we were walking in, the bouncer stopped us. This Hulk Hogan-looking-guy says, "Passes only." We then informed him that we didn't have any. He was kind, but let us know that the only way we were getting in was if we knew someone. You cannot gain entry into Heaven or know God without Jesus.

"Therefore he is able to save completely those who come to God through him, because he always lives to intercede for them." Hebrews 7:25 NIV

We spoke in the last section about Jesus as the full payment. This verse reinforces it and gives us a deeper understanding. When we see the concept of salvation fleshed out in scripture, we tend to see phrases like "through Him" and "in Him." There is no access to God apart from Jesus Christ. Even when Jesus came into this world and lived among people, He saw it as His mission to tell people this very thing:

"Jesus answered, "I am the way and the truth and the life. No one comes to the Father except through me.""
John 14:6 NIV

"He is 'the stone you builders rejected, which has become the cornerstone.' Salvation exists in no one else, for there is no other name under heaven given to men by which we must be saved." Acts 4:11-12 BSB

"No one" comes to God except through Christ.

That seems like an incredibly arrogant statement, but let us not forget Jesus is 100% God. He doesn't say that to be an arrogant statement, He says it because He loves us. Don't be tricked or fooled into thinking that you can gain access to God some other way. It only comes through accepting Jesus as your Lord and Savior. You may be saying, "But what about my neighbor, he's a great guy?" It is not about being good; the question is, do they know Jesus? Because He is the *only* way to God.

While reading this book, you may have realized that you've been counting on something else to get you to God. The separation cannot be bridged on your own. In order to gain access to God, you must place your hope and trust in Jesus.

PREACH JESUS EVERY TIME

I love playing basketball. Growing up, it was my favorite sport. I would like to tell you that I was incredible at the sport, but that would be a lie. I have always been a "well-rounded" Caucasian and we all know white men can't jump. If that last statement offended you, you missed a classic 1992 Wesley Snipes movie. Being well-rounded, my feet tend to stay on the ground, but one day I was dared to dunk. I am a sucker for a challenge, so I began to run from the three-point line and jumped but came up short.

I wasn't going to give up that easily, though, so I ran from half-court. A noble attempt, but still, I came up short. No matter what I did, I could never touch the rim. It was simply a gap that could not be bridged.

Spiritually you are a well-rounded white guy; no matter how fast you run, you just can't dunk. If we forget to preach Jesus, people will be getting close to the rim but missing it every time. When it comes to salvation, close is never close enough. You either have Jesus or you don't; there is no in-between. Our noble attempts to get to God can only be accomplished through Jesus.

> **You can come to church every week,** but it won't bridge the gap.
> **You can give,** but it won't bridge the gap.
> **You can be a good person,** but it won't bridge the gap.
> **You can serve,** but it won't bridge the gap.
> **You can read your Bible,** but it won't bridge the gap.

Only Jesus can bridge the gap sin created between you and God. The beauty of what you and I get to do as communicators of the Gospel is that we help people encounter Jesus. All of those things above are good things. Reading your Bible, serving, giving, and going to church are all great, but they are not what saves you. Those things are simply by-products of a relationship with Jesus Christ. When He is my Lord, I begin to love what He loves. I take on His personality and characteristics, and I am forever changed by it.

I believe that every time you and I teach God's Word, we should extend the opportunity for people to accept Jesus. It doesn't have to be long and overly complicated. You are simply facilitating a moment where people can respond to the promptings of God.

> *"Because, if you confess with your mouth that Jesus is Lord and believe in your heart that God raised him from the dead, you will be saved. For with the heart one believes and is justified, and with the mouth one confesses and is saved." Romans 10:9-10 ESV*

That verse shows us that leading people to Jesus is simple. Provide people an opportunity to confess with their mouth and believe in their heart. The prayer that you lead people through doesn't have to be overly complicated. Confession and belief are the only two things required for someone to be saved. When I teach, I like to have everyone in attendance say this prayer with me so that no one is left out. It also teaches them a prayer to use with others.

> "Dear Jesus, today I give You my life. I place my hope and trust in You. Thank You for dying in my place so that I can have new life. In Jesus' name, Amen."

There are some of you who realize that you have put your hope in things other than Jesus. Today you have the opportunity to surrender your life to Christ by confessing and believing that Jesus is the only way. If you need to make that decision, let's walk through a prayer together.

> "Dear Jesus, thank You for revealing to me that I have put my hope in things other than You. Today, I repent of my sin and believe that Your death was enough for me. Thank You for saving me!"

If you said that prayer, welcome to the family. Now go tell someone about the decision you just made! Know that your faith in Jesus was never intended to be private. Maybe the best way to start telling your story is to talk about where you were when God met you and how, through Jesus, you now have access to Him.

" ONLY JESUS CAN BRIDGE THE GAP SIN CREATED BETWEEN YOU AND GOD.

SECTION THREE

CHAPTER EIGHT

PREPARING TO PREACH

"Every time you expound a Bible text, you are not finished unless you demonstrate how it shows us that we cannot save ourselves and that only Jesus can."
- Tim Keller

"Work hard so you can present yourself to God and receive his approval. Be a good worker, one who does not need to be ashamed and who correctly explains the word of truth."
- 2 Timothy 2:15 NLT

We have now come to the final section of the book. I have enjoyed our journey so much thus far, but now is the time to give you some practical tools. The whole purpose of this book was not just for enjoyable reading, but for learning how to teach God's word on your own. I want to help you develop your own message within the framework and resources you have been given. These last few pages we have together will be more methodical than theological. This is simply what I have found most effective for me when it comes to message prep. The practical things that I am going to share are a starting point for you to figure out what works best for you. I hope that you find this next section helpful in your message development process.

A crucial part of delivering a message is the preparation. I once had a co-worker say, "If you fail to plan, you plan to fail." There are occasions where God just drops the perfect message into your lap. More often than not though, God meets us in our preparation and reading of His Word to give us a message to deliver. If you solely rely on God to speak to you in the final hour, you aren't a faithful steward of teaching scripture. Being led by the Spirit is not an excuse to neglect spending time in God's Word to prepare a message for His people. If God is the same yesterday, today, and forever then

He can meet me just as much in the planning as He can in the spontaneous. I want to walk you through my process for preparing sermon series and individual messages.

SERMON SERIES

If you aren't familiar with the concept, a sermon series is a collection of messages centered around a main idea, topic, or book of the Bible. When preparing a sermon series it's important to look at a few things:

What God is teaching you - As a communicator to people, I have found that God often teaches me things to deliver to other people. Ask yourself, "Is there a theme to what God is teaching you?" Maybe God is stretching your faith. You could be on the brink of a faith-based sermon series. Perhaps you have been walking through James in your own time. God may bring it full circle by having you develop a five week sermon series going through the book of James. Don't underestimate the power of what God is teaching you in this season. He may just be setting you up to deliver it to others in the next.

Calendar - I often let the calendar drive the development of sermon series' in our church. On the calendar for Propel Church, there are some big Sundays that we have every year. Sundays like Christmas, Easter, Mother's Day, Baptism, Church Birthday, and Small Group Kick Off. Here is how I think through our calendar:

January - People are in the mood for all things new, so in the month of January I try to do a series on new beginnings. We kick off 21 Days of Prayer & Fasting to refocus ourselves on God for the upcoming year. We also host a Baptism Weekend in January to give people the opportunity to take their next step in their new beginning.

February - In February, we have our spring semester of groups kick off and, for us, it's the perfect time to talk about relationships. Relationships in marriage, with friends, and with God. Valentine's Day falls right in the middle of this month so it's super easy to talk about what people are thinking about.

March - March can be tricky sometimes because Easter can fall later in the month but regardless, I try to lead people up to the cross. You can take people through Jesus' last moments before His death or this could be a great time to talk about evangelism.

April - Easter will normally fall in this month. People are way more likely to try church in this season. On Easter, we tend to focus on a simplistic gospel message where people can understand that God bridged the gap for them. Teach your people the importance of inviting during this season and lean into the momentum.

May - Rounding out April and into May, I like to do a topical sermon series that will pique interest in people. A highly engaging series can help the new people who came for Easter stick around. Think about the needs of your people and, if you don't know, ask! We also tend to leverage Mother's Day and a second quarter Baptism Weekend in May.

June - For us, June has Father's Day, Small Group Kick Off for summer semester, and it's the end of school. I have found that the summer is a difficult time for a sermon series due to travel schedules. During the summer, I like to just teach stand-alone messages, bring in guest speakers, and even play a video teaching from another pastor.

July - Since we aren't doing a message series, we use July to help people find a small group and we provide opportunities for people to get connected on Sundays. We use popsicles, watermelon, and more to help people hang out for a few extra minutes and talk to others. Don't slack off during the summer; it's a perfect time for people to find a new church.

August - In August, we kick off another round of 21 Days of Prayer but this time, no fasting. The purpose of this is to re-focus halfway through the year and end well. I think this is the perfect time to walk through a book of the Bible with people. Create a simple Bible reading plan and teach your people to fall in love with God's Word for themselves. Schools will be back in session, so people are creating rhythms again. For many people, attending church is one of the rhythms they want to solidify in the fall.

September - I love the month of September because for us, we celebrate the church's birthday. During this time, I lean heavily into a vision-oriented sermon series. I think of it as a time to "rally the troops," get people fired up about what all God has done, and release them into the next season. We also have another Baptism Weekend and Small Group Kick Off in this month to help people get connected.

October - October is an interesting month because it is around everything and nothing at the same time. I keep this open for whatever series I think will be most beneficial for our people at that time. I may do a series based on a book I have read that year or a topic that is close to my heart.

November - November is the beginning of the holiday season and as such, I like to talk about giving. People are already thinking about receiving, but the Kingdom of God is counter-cultural. We get to teach people that it is truly better to give than to receive.

Don't be scared to talk about money; you are hitting a heart issue for many.

December - The Christmas season is considered the most wonderful time of the year by some, but for many it is incredibly difficult. I like to teach people how to survive the holidays and share Jesus with their family. Christmas is also one of the other times of the year that people are more likely to show up to church. Remind people that every friend or family gathering is also an opportunity to share the Gospel and invite people to join them for a Christmas experience at your church.

INDIVIDUAL MESSAGES

Preparing individual messages doesn't have to be as complicated as we tend to make it. I remember hearing a professor say in a Hermeneutics course, "If you aren't spending at least 24 hours on a message, you aren't faithful to God's Word." In that moment, I remember feeling guilt and shame. When I looked at my work week, being a bi-vocational pastor, I didn't have 24 hours to dedicate to message prep. Should I just hang up my hat, quit, and shrink back into my former life before Christ? Absolutely not! So I developed a system that works for me in spending a large amount of time on every message. The trick is, you have to get good at planning messages months in advance.

I started with the sermon series portion first because for me, it starts with what God is speaking, followed by series development, which leads to message prep. I occasionally write stand-alone messages, but the most common way I prepare a message is in the framework of a sermon series. A sermon series is just a collection of individual messages, so I want to give you some practical things that I do while preparing those messages.

Here is what a vision series looks like at the church I pastor. We have four parts to our vision: Know God, Find Freedom, Discover Your Purpose, Make a Difference. This is not a unique vision to us; we are part of the "Grow Network" based out of Church of the Highlands. I would encourage you to take a look into the network if you are looking for practical tools to better lead your church and people. Below, I will walk you through a series outline and individual message prep.

Sermon Series Objective - Help people connect with the vision of our church in a way that fits in their life.

Week 1 - Know God (relationship with God; baptism)
Week 2 - Find Freedom (small groups)
Week 3 - Discover Your Purpose (spiritual gifts)
Week 4 - Make a Difference (serving)

1. Identify the sermon series along with main ideas for each week - Once you have the main objective for your series, start mapping out how many weeks it will be. Then move into what each week looks like. Make sure that your individual messages help fulfill whatever objective you have determined for your series.

2. Create an easily accessible notebook - When beginning the process, I start a digital notebook in my phone using an app called Evernote. A "notebook" in this app is just a sorting mechanism for individual notes. Your notebook should be titled the name of the sermon series or, if still in the development process, a theme.

3. Create individual notes - Once the notebook is created, I create individual notes for each sermon. I may label these notes with the title of the message or just the "(Sermon Series) - Week #."

4. Consistently add to the notes - God is consistently speaking to us not just as sons and daughters, but also as communicators. I start the process of adding notes to each sermon as they comes to mind.

I do not have the ability to spend 24 hours on an individual message, but with the right rhythm I can still be a good steward of scripture. For me, this method allows me to spend five to thirty minutes at a time to add things into my notes. When I sit down to put my notes together, it's a culmination of six months of listening to God speak on a topic. This method of sermon prep is what I call the "crock-pot method." When I first started teaching scripture, due to lack of time and inexperience, the messages I prepared seemed to come from a microwave. I would toss something together at the last minute and just hope that it turned out well. Now I slow cook what God is speaking, and I am proud of the dish served because I know what went into it. Each ingredient added at just the right time to craft the perfect dish.

Between preaching at our church, leadership teachings, and traveling to speak, I prepare around 100 messages per year. Here are some things I do that help with this process:

Keep things on "the cloud" - With the technological advancements we have, it is easier than ever to prepare messages. For me, I love that on my phone I can access things done on my tablet and computer. All of this is possible because I use an online platform for all of my notes. Using something like Evernote, Google Docs, or Apple Notes gives you the ability to prepare on the go with ease.

Base your current learning on future series/messages you will deliver - Due to the high volume of messages I prepare each year, what I read is based on what I will be delivering later. If I am delivering a group of messages on faith, I may pick up a book that deep dives into faith or dig into scripture to look at all the times faith is mentioned. If you know what you are doing in the future, preparing for it now is the rational thing to do.

> **BEING LED BY THE SPIRIT IS NOT AN EXCUSE TO NEGLECT SPENDING TIME IN GOD'S WORD TO PREPARE A MESSAGE FOR HIS PEOPLE.**

STUDYING SCRIPTURE

As you begin to prepare messages, the time you spend studying scripture is crucial. It is quite simple for us to just read scripture at a surface level but when you teach, you have to grow accustomed to deep-diving into God's Word. There are truths for you and I to unlock as we spend time digging into His Word. If you are like me, you have a desire to study and grow more but just don't know where to start. Here are a few things that can help you as you study God's Word:

Plan to Study - The pace of life is incredibly hard to keep up with and, if you are not careful, your study time will be swept away in the busyness. For me, it is crucial to put my study time on my calendar. It may seem ridiculous to schedule time with God but the truth is, you schedule what's important. I have planned time that I rarely shift because the time I spend studying matters. Create specific opportunities on your calendar to study scripture and spend time with God. That may mean that you give up going out for lunch, or you only watch one episode of *The Office* instead of four. You will thank me later.

Prepare to Study - Whenever I am going to study I need to make sure that I have the right tools for the job. A roofer wouldn't show up to a job without a ladder because you prepare for the assignment at hand. When sitting down to study scripture, I bring my Bible, study Bible, notebook, and an iPad.

If you don't have a study Bible in your life, you need one! These Bibles are designed to help you surpass surface level reading and deep-dive into God's Word. I also bring my iPad with me wherever I go because of a tool called "Logos." This software/app allows me to have access to multiple translations of scripture, original languages, books, commentaries, word studies, and more. I highly reccomend this tool for people who teach God's Word. Your tools don't have to look like mine, but you do need to walk into your study time prepared and expectant for God to speak.

Study Biblical Characters - If you are new to studying scripture, I recommend starting with the study of the people in the Bible. These were real men and women who God used powerfully and whose lives still speak to us today. You could follow Peter's life from fisherman to church planter. Perhaps you look at the life of Joseph to see him from the time he had a dream to the time it was fulfilled. Dig into what they went through to see God's promises fulfilled in their life. How did they struggle? What did they do to overcome those struggles? How do their lives point us to Christ, and help us become more Christ-like? These are questions I might ask myself as I look at the life of a biblical character.

Study a Book of the Bible - Studying a book of the Bible is how most scholars will say you should do it. Consider it "industry standard" for preachers and teachers. As you study a book of the Bible, you have the opportunity to slow down as you go verse by verse through the text. As you slow down, you are able to pick up on what the theme of the book is, what is happening before and after each verse, and see how it all flows together. The book of Galatians is by far one of my favorite books of the Bible. If you are looking for a great place start, give yourself one hour a day and one chapter in Galatians a day for six days. I do that at least once a year and God speaks through it uniquely every single time.

Study Context - As I have said before in this book nothing in scripture is there by accident; every word is intentional. Because of that, we need to dig into the why behind what is actually there. Studying the context may mean that you go look into who a specific book of the Bible was written for. An example of this would be that the Gospel of Luke seems to show us more of the humanity of Jesus and is written for more of a Gentile audience. You might be thinking, "Why does that matter?" When you understand Luke's audience and get to Luke 15, it changes the way you look at lost sheep. Jesus leaves those who are found (Jews) to go after that which is lost (Gentiles). They found out that God hadn't forgotten about them; He was pursuing them and desired to bring them into His family. That's the power of studying context, it brings to light what has been there the entire time.

Study for Confirmation - We all have ideas that pop into our head from time to time. One of the reasons I study scripture is to ensure that when I get ready to teach, I am not sharing just a good idea when I should be sharing a God-inspired truth. "The Lord told me" does not trump "the Bible says." If God has "told you" something that isn't supported by scripture, it's not Him. I run every thought or message point I am going to teach through this filter: Is this idea supported in multiple places of scripture? If I simply cherry-pick a verse to teach a man-made concept, I am not a faithful steward of scripture. Scripture should be the foundational thing that formulates our thoughts and opinions.

As you prepare to teach God's Word, I have no doubt that He will speak to you. Don't carry around the weight or pressure that you have to deliver a good word. God is more than capable to use the worst presentation to draw someone to repentance.

Allow God to speak to you in the preparation. He knows exactly what His people need to hear and when they need to hear it.

"IF GOD HAS "TOLD YOU" SOMETHING THAT ISN'T SUPPORTED BY SCRIPTURE, IT'S NOT HIM.

STARTING POINT

Often times I have found that the hardest thing to do is to actually start putting your notes together. In the next chapter we will cover how to build your message notes. Consider this a cheat sheet to kickstart your prep process to bridge the gap for your audience.

Message Title:_____

Primary Scripture:_____

Where are they? _____
_____

Where does God want them?_____
_____

What is the point of this message and how do I want them to apply it? _____
_____

How am I communicating that this is only possible through Jesus?_____
_____

Other thoughts: _____
_____
_____
_____

CHAPTER NINE

OUTLINES AND OUTCOMES

"The secret of a good sermon is to have a good beginning and a good ending, then having the two as close together as possible."
- George Burns

"All Scripture is breathed out by God and profitable for teaching, for reproof, for correction, and for training in righteousness, that the man of God may be competent, equipped for every good work."
- 2 Timothy 3:16-17 BSB

In 2011, just a few weeks after giving my life to Jesus, I had the chance to preach my first message for a church on a Sunday. I was so honored to have the invitation but to be honest, I had no clue how to put my notes together. I went to the internet and searched for whatever I could find. In this chapter, I want to help you put your notes together in preparation to teach. I hope to help you avoid those pitfalls that I experienced when first starting out. Before I prepare my notes there are two things that I do:

1. Pray - I cannot stress how important prayer is when you begin to put your notes together. The main prayer that I pray goes something like this: "God, I know that You love the people who will hear these words more than I do. I ask that You open my eyes and guide me through these notes so that people don't hear a word from me but from You!" You don't have to pray for three hours or even 30 minutes. You simply need to focus your mind and heart on the things of God. When we do that first, I have found that God pours out His greatest blessing over our work.

2. Resolve Your Takeaway - When preparing message notes, I like to make sure that I have figured out what I want those listening to leave with. It may be a singular thought or an overarching theme but, regardless, you need to think through it. If you don't have a target, you will miss every time. Making this decision will allow you to finish before you ever start preparing your notes. Knowing your endgame also ensures that all of your points and prep work have a cohesive feel. If my points and application don't align with what I want people to leave with, chances are it doesn't make it into the message.

MESSAGE NOTES

This next section is all about building your message notes. As we dive into this, I think that it's important for us to have a few guardrails before we enter. Below, I will put a passage of scripture and give you an example of how to structure your notes around it.

"Jesus, full of the Holy Spirit, left the Jordan and was led by the Spirit into the wilderness, where for forty days he was tempted by the devil. He ate nothing during those days, and at the end of them he was hungry. The devil said to him, "If you are the Son of God, tell this stone to become bread." Jesus answered, "It is written: 'Man shall not live on bread alone.'"" Luke 4:1-4 NLT

There are many reasons why I am a proponent of a 30-35 minute message, but truthfully it depends on your audience and church culture. Let's say that you live in the middle and are delivering a sermon for 32 minutes. In preparation, a message is broken into three parts.

Introduction - Where you are
(Connection - 7 minutes)
Body - Where God wants you to be; Planks
(Vision; Points & Application - 20 minutes)
Closing - Ropes (Jesus - 5 minutes)

There are so many ways to build your notes that it can feel overwhelming at times. I have listed a few primary ways that communicators all around the world prepare their notes.

Manuscript - Manuscript notes are a word-for-word way to structure your notes. Below is a manuscript example of a message from the passage of scripture in Luke 4:

"The first point I have for you this morning is 'We overcome sin through the power of the Holy Spirit.' In Luke chapter 4, the easy thing to do is teach on temptation. Was Jesus tempted in the wilderness?

Absolutely. However, in Luke chapter 3 we find the genealogy of Jesus traced all the way back to Adam. Adam, like Jesus, had been tempted but failed. In this passage, if Jesus caves into the temptation, He is not the Messiah because He would have sinned. Luke 4 begins by letting us know that Jesus was full of the Spirit when He was tempted. That is why He was able to overcome sin! It wasn't based on a Bible reading plan or by works, but by the Spirit of God within Him!"

I recommend the style of manuscript notes for new communicators. When you start teaching it's easy to get nervous and forget what you wanted to say. There is no shame in this method either, as many teachers feel it keeps them from drifting into false teaching and helps them stay true to what they prepared.

Outline - Outline format is a way to build your message notes in bullet points. If you are preaching through the Bible verse by verse, practice your message a lot, or are a very skilled communicator, an outline may work perfectly for you. Here is an actual message outline I used on a Sunday morning at the church I lead:

Intro

Luke 4:1-13

Hebrews 4:15

1. We all have a fight

Luke 3:38

2. We overcome sin through the power of the Holy Spirit

Romans 8:12

3. Fights prepare you for your purpose

Luke 4:18-19

Closing

Blend - After trying both manuscripts and outlines, I found that neither one of those really worked for me. So, I blended the two together to get the most out of my notes. When I teach, I lay things out in an outline format but place words or phrases to trigger thoughts. Here is an example:

Intro - Welcome | Vision | Story of fight

Luke 4:1-13 - Read straight through

Hebrews 4:15 - God relates with us by becoming us

1. We all have a fight - What fight are you in?

Luke 3:38 - Jesus is 2nd Adam

2. We overcome sin through the power of the Holy Spirit - Go back to verse 1

Romans 8:12 - I don't have to, I choose to

3. Fights prepare you for your purpose - Your pain isn't wasted

Luke 4:18-19 - The Spirit is upon you

Closing - Without Jesus, you are still obligated to sin

After looking at these three different ways to build your notes you may be wondering, "Which one is best?" The answer: whichever one works best for you. The person who benefits the most from the structure of your notes is you. My recommendation would be that you build your notes in a way that creates the least amount of distraction possible.

> **BUILD YOUR NOTES IN A WAY THAT CREATES THE LEAST AMOUNT OF DISTRACTION POSSIBLE.**

INTRODUCTION

Your introduction is the first opportunity you have to connect with your audience. Some may say it's not really important, but I have found you have the most attention from people in the first five minutes of a message. If your introduction isn't captivating, chances are your audience will tune out. The opposite is also true! Create a captivating introduction and you will have buy-in from your audience throughout the remainder of your delivery. There are many different ways to do an introduction. Feel free to use one of the options below:

Message Introduction #1: Humor

Humor is probably my favorite type of introduction because I believe many churches and Christians have been robbed of laughter. Telling a joke or using humor is a way to gain quick buy-in from your audience. For example, one of the stories I like to share took place at the gym: "I started my workout by running on a treadmill (which I hate) and everything was fine until a guy came running beside me. This incredibly buff man kept increasing his speed and then looking at me. I knew the race was on so I looked back and kept increasing my speed. It's a competition now. When I looked at him, my back foot hit my front foot and it sent me flying off the back of the treadmill. Yes, I became one of those fail videos."

Humor is an easy way to grab people's attention, but be sure that your jokes have a purpose. Use the irony and humor of a situation to connect with everyday life tension that your audience has faced. I drew people in with the funny story and then transitioned to say, "Sounds funny, but that day I learned that I will always trip watching someone else run their race. Today, I want to talk with you about comparison..."

Message Introduction #2: Facts and Stats

Often, I have found that we become desensitized to the darkness of the world around us. Using facts and statistics are a way to bring light to the reality that we live in. For example:

"One in three marriages will end in divorce."

"Two out of three men admit to watching porn once a week."

"If a Father comes to faith first, there is an 80% chance that his family does the same."

In your intro you can create some shock by inserting a real life statistic. Be sure that when you use statistics you cite your sources. Those who take notes will fact check you on the information you provide. I don't recommend making up these stats on the fly. If an unchurched person fact checks you on a stat and you falsified it, why should they believe what you say about God?

Message Introduction #3: Backwards Statements

One of my favorite sermon series we have ever done was called "Bad Advice." This series came from Pastor Craig Groeschel and the team at Life.church. They give away tons of resources to churches on the open.church network. When starting this series I said something like, "Today I'm going to teach you how to get stuck in an addiction." An opening statement like that will captivate your audience. Once you have their attention, it opens them up to receive what God has for them that day.

Message Introduction #4: Personal Stories

Telling an engaging story is one way to draw an audience in, and it's even better if you can make it personal. People want to be let into the real life moments that you've had so they know they aren't alone in their struggles. I enjoy sharing stories of my real life with people because it lets them see that I am a real person. You can share about the frustrations of airports, flat tires, food poisoning, funny moments with pets, traveling, moments with your kids, and more. Whatever you share with people, be sure to think through how they feel in those moments. Emotion is the thread that is woven through a great story. Hit the emotions that come with being cut off in traffic, losing a loved one, or your first child being born and you will invite your listeners into your journey.

Message Introduction #5: Captivating Questions

I think one of the reasons why people don't listen to us at times is that we are answering questions no one is asking. If you want to get the attention of people, toss out questions they or their friends are asking. It could be something like "If God is good, why do bad things happen?" or "How can a good and loving God send people to Hell?" The questions you ask should be a reflection of things people are thinking about. If you don't know, simply ask your people! They want to help you because it's a win for them as well. There is power in calling out the elephant in the room and going where some people aren't willing to go.

Message Introduction #6: Engaging Scriptures

If I am looking to come out swinging, the first thing I hit in my intro is an engaging passage of scripture like Psalm 22:1, "My God, my God, why have you forsaken me?" This type of introduction is one that I use least often because lost people tend to tune out. If you want to get their attention, be sure to bring out a passage of scripture that is really engaging and relatable. Go through the exercise we have talked about in meeting people where they are and select a passage of scripture where they can see that displayed.

BODY

The body of your notes will contain the majority of the content that you deliver. This is really the teaching portion of your message where your audience is going to learn from God's Word, apply it to their life, and then be released to live it out. This is where your content is going to live for your listener to receive. Here are a few filters that I run my content through while building my notes:

Sound - I have mentioned it throughout this book, but I believe that it is crucial that your notes are theologically sound. Scripture is clear that those who teach are held accountable for what is taught, so we know it matters to God as well. As I am building my notes, I am looking to make sure that nothing is just a good thought or opinion. I do not have permission by God to twist, contort, or even bend scripture to fit the agenda of the message I am delivering. As you sit down to structure your notes, be sure to go back to some of the study tips from the previous chapter. If God says it or reinforces it more than once, chances are you are onto something. If not, it might just be indigestion from something that you ate.

Simple - For a long time, pastors and leaders have done a really good job of making things more complicated than they need to be. As you look at formulating your points and application, strive for simplicity. Let your thoughts and ideas go through a phase of contraction until they are boiled down to the most simplistic way to say it. Making it simple doesn't mean you are watering it down, it means that you care so much about the people God has called you to that you want to make sure they get it. If you have been called by God to teach His word, you should learn to teach to kids. Kids ministry was the place that I fell in love with watching God's Word come alive in someone's life. I have never had a passion for kids ministry, but I do have a passion for helping people connect to God's Word. Don't overestimate the education level of your audience; you aren't there to impress people with your knowledge.

Practical - In Mark 5, Jesus is having a conversation with the rich young ruler and He says, "Go sell all of your possessions, then come follow Me." Jesus gave him something practical to do in order to follow Him. As you invest the time in preparing your notes, make sure that you are giving people practical things to run with. I like to think through the next steps that align with our vision as a church. In the message, I may challenge them this week to start a Bible reading plan or find a small group. My hope for a Sunday is getting someone to take a next step because each step is one step closer to God. People have the desire to change but often don't know where to begin. That's the power that you and I carry! We get to resource people who want to change with the tools necessary to make it happen.

Alignment - Nothing will make you lose your audience more than a ton of scattered thoughts that have nothing to do with each other. Identify where you want people to end up and then work backwards to ensure that there is alignment throughout the entire message. When I listen to a message that lacks alignment, it shows me a lot about their preparation process. Alignment is an incredibly important feature on a vehicle because it is the thing that keeps your car going in a straight direction. If you are out of alignment it is so easy to drift to the left or to the right of the road. Simply put, alignment brings clarity, cohesion, and the ability to stay on course with the message that God has entrusted you to deliver. Alignment allows you to stay in your lane and helps your audience continue on the journey with you. If you have a lot of good content but it doesn't all align with your outcome for an individual message, you may be on track for a sermon series. You may feel pressure to cram everything into one weekend but remember, this is a journey not just a stop.

Authentic - We live in a world that craves authenticity. They are seeking out, wanting, and desiring those who are willing to be real, transparent, and genuine. As Craig Groeschel says, "People would rather follow a leader who is real, than one who is always right." One of the greatest ways to be more authentic is to leverage the power of stories. Don't be afraid of telling stories that have taken place in your life, but make sure they don't stop with you. Your stories should point people to a deeper biblical truth you are trying to unpack. Whenever I tell stories in a message, I love to share my struggles or things that have taken place in my life. But at the end you need to transition it. It can start out with "I _____ ," but should end with "We _____."

One of the most inauthentic things you can do is stand on stage, point your finger and say, "You do _____" or "You are_____." Nope, authenticity says, "we struggle, we laugh, we cry." Make sure that people understand that we are no better than they are; God is working on and in each one of us.

CLOSING

The last portion of your notes is actually the most important. If you have gone through the process I have recommended, this part of your notes will actually come first. The reason why your closing matters so much is because, if messed up, it's what people are thinking about when they leave. As a person who flys a lot, my win for a flight is that I make it from point A to point B safely and efficiently. I was flying one day and the flight was almost perfect. The part that ruined it for me was the landing. The pilot ended up slamming the plane so hard on the runway that we bounced and went back up in the air to try again. An eight hour perfect flight was messed up in my eyes because of the last five minutes. The way you finish matters just as much as how you start! Here are a few things to think through while using the plane analogy:

Announce It - As a flight comes to an end, there is

an announcement by the pilot telling you that your flight is coming to a close. On the majority of the flights I have been on, the pilot even lets you know what your destination looks like. As you are closing out the message, let them know that your time together is ending. It could be as simple as saying, "Today as we wrap up our time together, remember that when you choose to forgive those who have hurt you, you experience God's preffered future for your life." For the love of all that is holy, don't tell people 17 times that you are wrapping up if you aren't. Telling people you are ending and choosing not to only creates misery in them.

Slow Down - When your flight is coming to an end you must decrease your speed. I have watched sermons where pastors rush the ending (normally because they wasted valuable time early on) and because of it, the ending is rough and abrupt. People accepting Jesus as their Lord and Savior is the *most* important thing you will do, so don't rush it. Slow down the pace of your closing to make sure that people are understanding who Jesus is and what He did for them. Landing the plane smoothly creates an excellent experience at the end.

Funnel Them To A Decision - After the plane

lands, people begin to unbuckle, get out of their seat, and grab their carry-ons. In order to exit the plane, they had to make a decision to get up and do something, even if it's just walk. Every time you preach make sure that you are bringing people to a moment where they are making a decision. In my opinion, there are two main decisions people need to make: salvation and sin removal. First, invite those who do not have a relationship with Jesus to begin one. Then address those who are listening that need to lay specific sin issues down. You have slowed down to make sure they understand Jesus and now it's time to do something with it. One of my favorite things Pastor Chris Hodges says is, "Choices lead, feelings follow." Let's help people make decisions today!

Transition - As they exit the plane, people head into many different directions to go their own way. When you end a message, you are sending people out to wherever God has placed them. At our church, once I am done teaching, I end in prayer and then talk about the next song we are doing. Some end with a benediction, which is simply the speaking of a blessing over your people that is supported by scripture. Regardless of how you wrap things up, make it as smooth as possible. Distraction free environments help people stay focused on God.

POTENTIAL OBSTACLES

In my years in ministry I can confidently say that I have written over 200 messages. I would love to tell you that in doing so, I have figured out a way to do it perfectly every time. Unfortunatley, I cannot. There are obstacles, but thankfully they seem to be consistent. Below are three common obstacles that I tend to face when developing my message notes.

Creativity block - In ministry and message prep there are high seasons and dry seasons. When I am in the high season, I find that I can write messages like I write text messages. In the dry seasons though, I tend to run into a creative block. I become paralyzed by my lack of ideas on a particular topic.

Tip: Remember you are a problem solver. When you teach, you identify where people are and help them get to where God wants them to be. When I look at it from that perspective, my role as a communicator is as simple as solving a problem or showing people how a gap can be bridged.

Too little content - On Saturday nights, I run through the entire message for Sunday mornings.

More often than I would like to admit, I end up with too little content to teach. I will never forget the night I ran through what I thought would be a 35 minute message and finished it in 18.

Tip: Take your content through the process of expansion. When I come up with too little content, I start looking at what I have and try and figure out how to zoom out. How can I make this message larger? It may be a relatable story or another supporting verse. No matter what I add, it must reinforce the message I am trying to communicate.

Too much content - On the flip side of having too little content, there are times that I have way too much content. It isn't cause for celebration to have 35 minutes to teach but execute it in 42. It's dishonorable to your audience because time is something you can take from someone that they can't get back.

Tip: Take your content through the process of contraction. Take a look at your points, stories, and content and attempt to figure out a way to say it better, in less time. An example would be telling people about the five verses before a main passage of scripture rather than reading it. If you have too much content, break it into multiple messages.

"PEOPLE ACCEPTING JESUS AS THEIR LORD AND SAVIOR IS THE MOST IMPORTANT THING YOU WILL DO, SO DON'T RUSH IT.

CHAPTER TEN

TIPS FOR COMMUNICATORS

"You can preach a better sermon with your life than
with your lips."
- Oliver Goldsmith

"My goal is that they may be encouraged in heart and
united in love, so that they may have the full riches of
complete understanding, in order that they may know
the mystery of God, namely, Christ, in whom are hidden
all the treasures of wisdom and knowledge."
- Colossians 2:2-3 NIV

If you have been following the process of *Bridge the Gap*, you now have planned and developed notes for a message. Congratulations! Often, the hardest part is just getting started. Here are some things I do each week that have helped me in the delivery of a message:

Practice the Message - I can't stress this enough. It is so important that you run through your mes-sage ahead of time. You will find me Saturday night around 8pm in my office practicing. I also take ad-vantage of car rides when I am by myself to just talk through what I have written down.

Get Sleep - If you wake up exhausted, chances are that it will carry into your delivery. Plan on going to bed early to get a great night's sleep before you teach. For me, that means that I am not going out or staying up on Saturday nights because how rested I am on Sunday, matters.

Download/Print Your Notes - On Sundays I teach from an iPad, but I have learned the value of having my notes also printed. There is nothing more terrifying than getting on stage to teach only to find a low battery on your device. No one will like you any less for teaching with notes, so figure out what works best for you.

Stay Hydrated - Hydration is so important for you to be able to effectively communicate the message God has given you. When I started teaching more frequently there were specific drinks that I cut out due to what it did to my throat. If needed, have a bottle of water with you while you teach.

Pick Three People - People can make you incredibly nervous when you are teaching. It's hard to deliver God's Word and stare into the eyes of the guy who looks mad that he is there. I like to pick three people (at our church, that is one per section) to look at while I teach. It makes people in the audience feel like I look at every section, while minimizing distractions for myself.

Rewatch Your Message - Every Monday I take time to rewatch the message I have delivered the previous weekend. It gives me the opportunity to celebrate the things I did well and critique that which could be better. If you aren't on video, simply hit the audio recorder on your phone to listen back later. Doing this has been one of the most beneficial things in my development as a communicator.

EIGHT THINGS I WISH I HAD KNOWN

When I was thinking about how to conclude this book, I wanted to resist the temptation to tell you how to stand on the platform to teach. It would be arrogant for me to deduct that my way is the best or only way to do it. I just wanted to present a model that helps you more in the preparation than anything else. The truth is, on a communication spectrum, there are so many who have executed it longer and better than I. Below are eight tips that I wish someone had shared with me when I started. These things are not exclusive to just teaching, they are lessons that have shaped the man of God I am today.

1. Don't let your time with Jesus become message prep

Perhaps the most unfortunate of pitfalls so many pastors fall into is depleted time with God. Spending time with God and spending time preparing messages are not the same thing. One is development of relationship and the other is the external expression of your faith lived out. I have fallen into this trap more times than I would like to admit and the results are always low energy, lack of passion, and minimized joy. In those times, my focus fell off of God and onto my ability to perform. It reminds me of the prodigal son in Luke 15:

> *"'I will set out and go back to my father and say to him:*
> *Father, I have sinned against heaven and against you. I*
> *am no longer worthy to be called your son; make me like*
> *one of your hired servants.'" Luke 15:18-19 NIV*

This young man had position in the family but was going to just come work for his father. Servants work, but sons sit. Never forget that you are a son or daughter of God before you are a teacher or preacher. There is a time to work, but works don't come before growing in your relationship with our Heavenly Father.

2. Find your own voice

As I write this book in 2019, I have the ability to gain access to the teachings of thousands of pastors and Bible teachers. Videos of preachers are going viral and the easy thing to do is try and teach or preach like someone else. But it will never work.

> *"Then Saul dressed David in his own tunic. He put a coat*
> *of armor on him and a bronze helmet on his head. David*
> *fastened on his sword over the tunic and tried walking*
> *around, because he was not used to them."I cannot go in*
> *these," he said to Saul, "because I am not used to them."*

So he took them off. Then he took his staff in his hand, chose five smooth stones from the stream, put them in the pouch of his shepherd's bag and, with his sling in his hand, approached the Philistine." 1 Samuel 17:38-40 NIV

Hey David, or whatever your name is, stop trying to wear Saul's armor. Stop trying to teach like Pastor Steven Furtick, tell stories like Pastor Judah Smith, and create outlines like Pastor Chris Hodges. Each time you do that, you walk into battle wearing someone else's armor. There is a unique voice that God is crafting within you. Find it and own it!

"THERE IS A UNIQUE VOICE THAT GOD IS CRAFTING WITHIN YOU. FIND IT AND OWN IT.

3. Develop a healthy prayer life

Prayer is most effective when it's a lifestyle we cultivate rather than something we do every now and then. To understand how to have a lifestyle of prayer, we can look at the example Jesus gave during His life on earth.

"Very early in the morning, while it was still dark, Jesus got up, left the house and went up to a solitary place, where He prayed." Mark 1:35 NIV

Pick a time - Jesus got up early in the morning to spend time with His Heavenly Father. Make a daily appointment with God and faithfully keep it, whether it's first thing in the morning, at lunch, or in the evening.

Find a place - Jesus had a special place where He went to pray. Having a designated place to pray helps us remove distractions and frees us to worship and pray out loud.

Have a plan - When Jesus taught His disciples how to pray, He gave them a prayer outline. We call it The Lord's Prayer. That outline is available in chapter six of this book, if you want to go back through it. When we pray every day, our plans for our prayer time can vary. It may include worship music, Bible reading, and quiet time to listen to God. It doesn't always have to look the same, it just helps when we have a plan for connecting regularly with God.

4. Listen to other communicators

I mentioned that you need to find your own voice, but please don't stop listening to other voices. On our team I am consistently asking our people who they are listening to because I can't be the only voice they hear. God uses other people to impart His truth to us in ways we may have never seen before. Take some time today and find some other communicators of the Gospel that you can start listening to. I don't buy into the thought that we have to agree on everything in order for me to listen to you. If God can speak through a donkey, I know He can use the gifts He placed in other pastors. So as I sit down to listen to someone open scripture, I pray this verse over my time:

> *"If you need wisdom, ask our generous God, and he will give it to you. He will not rebuke you for asking."*
> *James 1:5 NLT*

When you and I choose to listen to others I believe that God supernaturally imparts His wisdom to us.

5. You are not exempt from Sabbath rest

About three years into ministry, God began speaking to me about my "Sabbath." In all honesty, I had heard my dad talk about the Sabbath being on Sunday so that's what I did. Except I am in ministry, and Sunday is the furthest thing from a day of rest for me. I love what I get to do, but when I look at a Sunday I view it as a day where I run 200mph in efforts to help lost people meet Jesus. Being a pastor, teacher, or even just a follower of Jesus doesn't exempt you from taking a Sabbath.

"But the seventh day is a sabbath to the LORD your God..." Deuteronomy 5:14 CSB

God created us with the ability to accomplish all we are called to do in six days not seven. Don't believe me? Go back and look in the book of Genesis. God rested not because He was tired, but because He chose to rest. You and I are made to rest; here is the rhythm of rest that I strive for:

1 day for every 7 days
1 weekend for every 7 weeks

1 week for 7 months

1 month for every 7 years

I am not perfect and do make mistakes with this, but I feel more alive in my walk with Christ when I stick with this rhythm. One more note: my Sabbath time is not the same as my vacation time. Vacation is for my family, Sabbath is for my relationship with God.

6. Preach from your scars, not your wounds

If you have lived for any amount of time, chances are that you have been wounded. The difference between a scar and a wound is *healing*. As a young communicator, I didn't realize that in efforts to be transparent I actually bled all over people. People don't like to be and don't need to be bled on. Your audience is not the proper place to vent or dump your issues.

> *"Therefore confess your sins to each other and pray for each other so that you may be healed. The prayer of a righteous person is powerful and effective."*
> *James 5:16 NIV*

The proper place for you to deal with your sin issue is a smaller group of people. Have a healthy habit of confession and God will turn wounds into scars. Then as you teach, it's from a place of healing rather than hurt.

7. Learn to love feedback

After each message I deliver, I ask those I trust for honest feedback. It's important not to seek feedback for the purpose of receiving a "you did amazing." I seek feedback because I deeply care about lost people and if teaching better can make it easier for people to see Jesus, I am all for it. Feedback is vital to being a healthy communicator because it places you in a state of continual improvement.

"Listen to advice and accept instruction, that you may gain wisdom in the future." Proverbs 19:20 ESV

To be honest, in the beginning, receiving feedback from people was weird. I got really defensive about what I did or the way I did it but now things are different. I look at the feedback and assess how I can do things better in the future.

8. Remember this is a marathon not a sprint

I saved this one for last because it is the one I forget the most. Often, I get so caught up in the little moments of life I forget that I am not running a sprint. A sprint requires great acceleration, but a marathon requires endurance. Unfortunately, I know more people who have walked away from ministry than those still in it. Running this as a sprint will lead to striving, exhaustion, and burnout. But there is a better way:

"Therefore, since we are surrounded by such a great cloud of witnesses, let us throw off everything that hinders and the sin that so easily entangles. And let us run with perseverance the race marked out for us, fixing our eyes on Jesus, the pioneer and perfecter of faith. For the joy set before him he endured the cross, scorning its shame, and sat down at the right hand of the throne of God. Consider him who endured such opposition from sinners, so that you will not grow weary and lose heart."
Hebrews 12:1-3 NIV

The better way to run is with perseverance and endurance. Drop the weight you may be feeling to accomplish in four years what took most 40. Drop the pressure of having to perform in front of people so that they love you. Let go of any sin you may be holding onto and in doing so, you will finish the race God has marked out for you! Every time you feel like giving up, remember what God did for you through Jesus. His perseverance affords us the ability to press on when things get tough.

CLOSING PRAYER

God, thank You for the opportunity to take the journey with this reader. I pray blessing and favor over them as they give their life to Your work. Instill passion and purpose in us to see lost people encounter their loving Heavenly Father. I thank You for the opportunity to grow as communicators of the good news of Jesus. And ask that we never strive for the approval of others as we teach. We rest as sons and daughters of the King, knowing that Your Kingdom will prevail above all else. I am believing that more people will say yes to Jesus as we show them the gap You bridged for them. You get all the glory, honor, and praise. In Jesus' name, AMEN!

CONNECT WITH ME

SOCIAL

Facebook: @realpsnicknewman
Instagram: @psnicknewman

BOOKING

Visit www.nicknewman.com
Email: hello@nicknewman.com

OTHER RESOURCES

RAISING UP
COMMUNICATORS

How to use Bridge the Gap to raise up communicators

DOWNLOAD NOW

www.nicknewman.com/bridgethegap

SMALL GROUP

How to use Bridge the Gap in a small group

DOWNLOAD NOW

www.nicknewman.com/bridgethegap

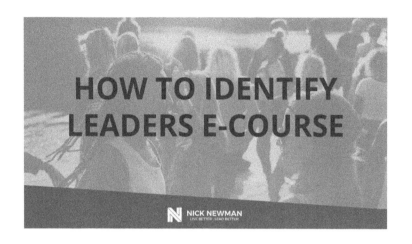

FIND THE RIGHT LEADERS

When we first started Propel I found myself wanting to raise up new leaders, but I had no clue where to start. After three years of building leadership pipelines and watching people step into different levels of leadership, I was ready to share some things I had learned. This course is designed to help you learn how to identify leaders in your organization with simple and practical tips. Take your next step today by purchasing the Identifying Leaders e-course!

Course Overview:
Session 1 – Hardships in Identifying Leaders
Session 2 – Finding the Right Leaders
Session 3 – Faithful Leaders
Session 4 – Available Leaders
Session 5 – Teachable Leaders
Session 6 – Inviting Leaders on the Journey

Purchase now at www.nicknewman.com

Made in USA - North Chelmsford, MA
1064619_9781699000700
03.30.2020 1027